Finding God
Is In
The Darkness

Twelve accounts of God's care through difficult times

Edited by Irene Howat

Christian Focus

© Christian Focus Publications

ISBN 1 85792 121 6

Published in 1998 by
Christian Focus Publications, Geanies House,
Fearn, Ross-shire, IV20 1TW

Cover design by Donna Macleod

Scripture quotations are from the New
International Version, unless otherwise stated.

CONTENTS

ACKNOWLEDGMENT

It has been a privilege to gather together, from among my friends and acquaintances, fifteen people who are prepared to share their experience of God's faithfulness to his promise never to leave them nor forsake them. Each has gone through adversity, and all have found God true to his word. I wish to thank them.

Irene Howat

FOREWORD

Jesus took the blind man of Bethsaida by the hand and led him out of the town (Mark 8:22-26). He led him out of the village, away from his friends, away from the familiar sounds and smells. He led him into territory that was unknown and frightening to the blind man. Each step made him more dependent on this stranger. Only the firm but gentle hold that Jesus had on him kept him going.

Sometimes in the midst of perplexing situations – in sorrow, in bereavement, in fear, in anxiety, in depression – Jesus leads his people into the unknown where they are alone with him; where their very solitude in the midst of pain, anguish of heart and tears blows the lid off their Christianity; when their eyes are opened to see Jesus as they have never seen him before.

There are times when we may be surrounded by family and friends and yet be alone, so alone, in the darkness of the turmoil of our breaking heart. The widow knows it when the mourners have gone home; the sick person knows it on the night before the operation; the parent knows it on the night of a phone call which tells of a loved one lost in a far off foreign land. But just as the artist uses dark shades to complete the picture, so the Lord in his providence uses the shadows of life to show us more of the divine picture of Jesus reaching out his mighty hand to sinful man. It is in the darkness that we hear his voice most clearly: 'Lo, I am with you alway' (Matthew 28:20, AV).

It is in the shadows that we evaluate things correctly and jettison useless baggage. The learning process must go on – there is much shaping to be done – Heaven's chisel has much to chip away to make us fit for glory. In one of George Macdonald's books we read of a woman, struck by a sudden sorrow, bitterly exclaiming, 'I wish I had never been made.' 'My dear,' said her friend, 'you are not made – you are being made and this is part of the Lord's process.'

> 'I walked a mile with Pleasure
> She chattered all the way,
> But left me none the wiser
> for all she had to say.
> I walked a mile with Sorrow
> And ne'er a word said she.
> But Oh the things I learned from her
> when sorrow walked with me.'

In this book Irene Howat has gathered together, in her usual sensitive way, twelve honest, moving experiences of ordinary men and women who have walked in the shadows of life and have felt the reassuring hand of the Man from Galilee.

I thoroughly recommend this book as it deals with realities.

Kenny MacDonald
January, 1998

CONTRIBUTORS

PAT CARDY

Pat Cardy and her husband, Andrew, live in Northern Ireland. They are parents and grand-parents. Pat and Andrew are used to 'the Troubles' there. But they went through a troubled time such as most of us cannot begin to imagine. In 1981, when their daughter Jennifer was nine years old, she left home to cycle to a friend's house to play. Jennifer never came back. A week after her disappearance her body was found. Jennifer had been murdered. The person responsible has never been found. Pat discovered that God's grace is sufficient for every need – even for the facing of her daughter's murder.

ELIZABETH AND DONALD MACKAY

Elizabeth and Donald live in Edinburgh. They have three grown up children. After a lifetime spent making herself available to help and support other people, over the course of just a few years Elizabeth became the one needing help. And Donald, who began his retirement by going back to studying, now finds himself as her full-time carer. In 1990 Elizabeth was diagnosed as suffering from degeneration of the cerebellum. She is now confined to a wheelchair; her sight, hearing, touch and ability to move have all been adversely affected. Their story is one of great weakness, and even greater strength.

JOHN MEIKLEJOHN

John is a retired prison governor. He and his wife, Irene, are happily settled in rural Scotland, with a garden that occupies much of their time. Living in one house for long is something of a novelty for them as John's job involved many moves. Such mobility makes for problems, some of which he shares with us. As a prison officer John met many and varied situations, from requests for both prayer meetings and pantomimes, to assisting in arranging some final visits for one of the last men to be executed in Scotland. John's account of life in the Prison Service is both challenging and heart warming.

KAY REID

Kay and her husband had four children and fostered others. As far as she was concerned, hers was the ideal marriage. Sadly, Kay's husband betrayed the sanctity of their marriage, leaving to live with another woman. The children were teenagers at the time. Kay had to cope with their shock, anger and hurt, while trying to survive her own. Faced with what seemed an impossible task, she set about providing for her family and bringing them up in the faith. Life is still a struggle. But

Kay has had the immense pleasure of seeing God work forgiveness in the lives of her children despite all that life threw at them.

KENNETH STEVEN

Kenneth is a young Scottish writer of undoubted ability. The hundreds of poems and several books he has had published bear witness to this. But making a living is not easy. Ken's Christian integrity refuses to allow him to compete with other writers on their terms. He writes of what is human and wholesome and true, refusing to conform to the nihilistic writing which is the norm for his generation today. This does not make him popular with either publishers or other writers. But there is a desire for wholesome writing as Kenneth discovered when a national newspaper printed an article of his on the subject.

LENA COWIE

Lena and her husband, Alex, live and work in Glasgow. Alex is engaged in Christian ministry there. All of their children are special, but Lena's account is of their son David, who is thirteen years old. David has some remarkable gifts. He has a zany sense of humour and a memory which never forgets a name or a face. However, David also has Cerebral Palsy, and is quadriplegic as a result. Lena describes her son's struggle from his earliest days to the present time. David cannot walk but he can get around. He has watched the birds fly off Orcadian cliffs and fed cows on a croft in Migdale. He's quite a boy.

RACHEL AND KATE

Rachel and Kate are sisters. When they were aged just three and five, their father left home. They are adults now, and look back over the years seeing how their parents' separation, and eventual divorce, affected them. Having found the loss of their father to be akin to bereavement, the sisters, while still young, had to face their mother's illness and death. The break-up of their parents' marriage left scars. But, far from indulging in self pity, Rachel and Kate have grown into caring and compassionate women, who hope the sharing of their experience will help readers better understand children who have lost a parent for whatever reason.

VERNON HIGHAM

Vernon and his wife, Morwen, live in Cardiff and are parents and grandparents. Vernon is pastor of Heath Evangelical Church and is a well known preacher on both sides of the Atlantic. Over twenty years ago, sudden serious ill health struck and it looked for a time as if Vernon's ministry was over and his life short. For fifteen years his life centred round coping with *status asthmaticus*. Preaching was a challenge, and holidays a nightmare.

Despite Vernon's restrictions God has greatly blessed his ministry in Cardiff. After a particularly bad time, God graciously removed Vernon's affliction. Now he and Morwen are enjoying their 'bonus years'.

ESMÉ DUNCAN
Esmé lives in Aberdeenshire. For much of her life she has seen singleness as an asset. It allowed her to give up a career in teaching and become a Scripture Union Staff Worker, with all the travelling that involved. Esmé's father had died when she was a student, and it was when her mother died that singleness became a problem. Being alone suddenly meant being lonely. It is with great honesty that Esmé takes us through her experiences: sharing the down times, the long climb up, and her eventual restoration to a point where, once again, singleness brings positive contentment. We also meet Mungo, her canine companion.

JONATHAN LAMB
Jonathan, who was brought up in London, now lives with his wife, Margaret, and their three daughters in Oxford. He serves as Regional Secretary for Europe and the former USSR for the International Fellowship of Evangelical Students. Currently he is also Chairman of the Keswick Convention. Jonathan suffered from polio as a child and has been left with a degree of

13

restriction in his mobility. While his walking is limited, Jonathan's flying is not! His job involves travelling for about 20 weeks of each year. He has written several books. Jonathan shares some challenging thoughts on coping with problems.

KATIE MORRISON

Katie, who died soon after completing her contribution to this book, was English but adopted Scotland as her own. After studying at Bible college she worked in a drug and alcohol rehabilitation centre. It was there Katie met the man she married. They had problems right from the start. Her husband, who was a recovering alcoholic, committed a serious offence and was imprisoned for life. Katie retrained then worked as a probation officer, cared for her elderly and disabled mother, and regularly travelled hundreds of miles to visit her husband. She died following surgery for a heart condition that had dogged her life.

JENNY AND ALASTAIR BROWN

Jenny and Alastair are living in Kintore in Aberdeenshire – for the second time. When they first stayed there Alastair was a draftsman. God then called him into the ministry and, after studying in Aberdeen, he moved with his wife and two sons, Andrew and Colin, to Ballater where he became minister of Glenmuick Church. Just

14

sixteen months after his ordination Alastair developed ME (*Myalgic Encephalomyelitis*). Three and a half years later, when still in his forties, he resigned from the ministry because of ill health. Jenny became the breadwinner, and Alastair uses his very limited energy in looking after their home.

1

PAT CARDY

It has been said that out of all our days there are fewer than fifty of which we have any clear remembrance; indeed, for most of us, perhaps half that number – our first day at school, a frightening awakening from a dreadful nightmare, the first time we met our life's partner, the death of a loved one, our graduation, our wedding day, a new job, a special holiday, the birth of our children – not many. Amidst these, some funny, some frightening, some sad and some very happy – all of which can be summoned up speedily and vividly – is one which needs no recollection for me. This one stands alone.

The 12th August 1981 was one of those laid back, nothing urgent days of school holiday. It should have been like the one before and, in all probability, the one to come – nice. Mark was thirteen, at secondary school, and more often than not arranged to cycle to his friend John's house to spend the afternoon there with his friends. That day there were more plans made. Jennifer was to cycle to her friend's house to play. Louise lived just over a mile away. I was content to let her do this. After all, hadn't she shown me how ably she could ride her bike along the road? It was a quiet country road with little traffic. Philip, only six, was looking forward to a trip to the swimming pool with John and his mum, Alma, my neighbour.

A feeling of foreboding

Why could I not get rid of the cold clammy feeling of depression that seemed to envelope me? My husband, Andrew, had sensed this too. In Ulster we were in the middle of 'The Troubles'. No-one knew who would 'get it' next – soldiers, UDR men, policemen, recently some business men, and always the public. Only the week before, Andrew, in partnership in his own business, had assured me that if anything happened to him he had provided adequate insurance for us all. I put such frightening thoughts away quickly.

So it happened that I was left that afternoon with the newest member of our family. Victoria was just eight months old, having been brought home from hospital two days before Christmas. That was a wonderful Christmas with four children, one of them newborn. My thoughts went heavenward as they had done so often. 'Thank you, dear Father, for this child. I don't understand it, but I love you for what you've done.' God had given Victoria to us in rather exceptional circumstances – fifteen months after I was sterilized! Even that had been taken out of our hands. 'As for God, his way is perfect' (2 Samuel 22:31, AV). I looked at that little one often and wondered why God in his sovereignty had given her in such a way. Today as I look back, why should this surprise me? Had he not proved himself able for me at every turn since I was converted? Now I know in larger measure what everlasting love really means. God loves us today and, because he loves us equally tomorrow, he deals with each of our days to provide for the need of our tomorrows.

I was only twenty one years old, married with a baby son, when the Lord lovingly and grandly stepped in through the door I had opened in my heart, coming with these words that were to mean so much to me over the years, 'Behold, I stand at the door and knock: if any man hear my voice, and open the door, I will come in to him, and will sup with him, and he with me' (Rev 3:20, AV). God showed me, on the one hand his majesty and glory, and on the other his immense love in not only dying for me, but making a solemn promise to commit himself to me through thick and thin, and to share all with me and I with him. 'I will sup with him and he with me.'

The nightmare begins

That afternoon saw our peaceful, happy world collapse. When Jennifer did not come home at her usual time of 4.30 pm, I had an uncanny sense that something was wrong. When Andrew came home I waited impatiently as he had his dinner and fixed a puncture on my car. 'Och, Pat, she's enjoyed her day and has likely stayed for tea,' he reassured me. But I knew she would have let me know. Leaving Andrew with the children, I soon found out she had never reached her friend's house, nor had anyone seen her. I tried to blanket the rising fear and panic with the realistic thought that she must be somewhere. We would soon find her. It was now 6.30 pm ... where could she be? Andrew and Wesley, our friend and neighbour, searched the district. Sitting outside under a tree in the garden holding Victoria I could voice no prayer. To put my desperate fears into audible words was to acknowledge, somehow, a nightmare that surely wasn't happening. But it was happening. And I did pray – choked unmemorable prayers.

Jennifer, a happy and sensible nine-year-old, was a delight to have around. She was a very loving child, full of fun and with an admirably positive nature, she soon dispelled any gloom she came in contact with! She was born a year and a half after we lost a stillborn son. I well remember, in answer to prayer for her safe arrival, the Lord giving me this precious verse, 'he hath blessed thy children within thee' (Psalm 147:13, AV). For so she proved to be, both blessed and a blessing. Saved when only six years old, I learned afterwards that she had gone to school saying, 'I'm saved and I'm going to heaven.' She loved to hear about heaven and kept a quiet time with her Lord until that very morning before she left.

Police were called and it soon became evident there was little more we could do. Just before midnight her bicycle was found half a mile from our house. It had been put over a hedge into a field. Andrew and I could only fall into each other's arms and cry.

It was then that I became aware of a strength that was not mine, that God in heaven was still my God, and that he was still sovereign, even then. This 'unnatural' peace was to override my benumbed emotions as I sought to shelter in him, not only for myself and my young family, but especially for my husband who was still unsaved.

Darkness without and within

That first night we did not sleep at all, and the second very fitfully and from sheer exhaustion. The next night saw me awake, alone, in the dark hours. The house was dark and outside even darker as I stood at our kitchen window in tears. I looked at the tree-lined horizon desperately seeking God who had never once let me down. But this was a God I didn't know any more! 'O God, why don't you tell us where she is? You are the only one who can help.' That night I think I feared for my sanity. Was she never to be found? Was

21

she alive or dead? And where was God? Had he left me too?

As I am diabetic the doctor called the following day and, because of the trauma of the previous night, he left me sleeping tablets. That night, after another anxious and heartbreaking day with no affirmative reports from any of the search parties, I took myself to bed with my tablets. What did the future hold? Perhaps this was the beginning of dependence on these! Each day I was drawing strength from *Daily Light*, a little book of selected Bible verses, learning to trust God because he was God. 'Surely God is my salvation; I will trust and not be afraid' (Isaiah 12:2). I looked at the tablets and felt an indignation that led me to seek God and his help alone. Some minutes later there stole into my heart the words of a psalm. 'It is vain for you to rise up early, to sit up late, to eat the bread of sorrows, for so he giveth his beloved sleep' (Psalm 127:2, AV). As I thought upon these words, and the love of my Heavenly Father, I claimed them for myself and slept peacefully, not only that night but every following one until this day. Isn't it just like God to put his finger on the point of our need and teach us to trust him when trusting is the hardest thing to do! He was showing me the reality of what I already knew. 'He lifted me out of the slimy pit, out of the mud and mire; he set my feet on a rock and gave me a firm place to stand' (Psalm 40:2).

Every night since Jennifer disappeared, a short epilogue service had been held in our house for all who gathered to support us and for those who had joined the search parties that day. These meant a lot to both Andrew and me.

'We only had the lend of her'
The following Tuesday, after having been missing for a week, Jennifer's body was found by two anglers. She had been murdered – strangled and drowned in a dam thirteen miles from our home. Words fail me to describe, even after all these years, the full horror of those awful moments when I knew all hope was gone. My recollection of that afternoon is vague now, and for that I'm thankful. That night in bed Andrew said these words, 'Pat, she's gone. We only had the lend of her.' How we had loved her.

The next few days were fraught. Andrew had to identify the body, a post-mortem was undertaken, and funeral preparations set in motion. But I feared the funeral itself. This would be the first I would see her brought home since the day Jennifer left so happily. The funeral was to be held in the garden of our home, in the warmth of an August afternoon. Having many relations, friends, neighbours, and strangers too, to comfort and help meant so much to us. My greatest fear, however, was setting my eyes on the reality of death – her coffin. Upon advice, and at our own request, the coffin was sealed. I think everything within us recoils at such a time. Death was never meant to be. Even Jesus 'was deeply moved in spirit and troubled', and wept in the presence of death (John 11:33).

My fearfulness ... God's faithfulness

That morning, full of many comings and goings, I secluded myself in our bathroom. That was, I had found, the safest place to pray without interruption. 'Dear Father,' I prayed, 'I just know you will uphold me as only you can do, but now I need you as I've never needed you before. I'm frightened.' I heard no audible voice, but just as clearly came these words, 'Go and look in your Bible. Look at where you had last read.' Up until then I could not read my Bible, being unable to concentrate. I obtained all I needed from *Daily Light*. Slipping upstairs I read these wonderful words: 'For our light affliction, which is but for a moment, worketh for us a far more exceeding and eternal weight of glory; while we look not at the things which are seen, but at the things which are not seen: for the things which are seen are temporal; but the things which are not seen are eternal' (2 Corinthians 4:17-18, AV).

This seared and sealed itself to my heart as only the Word of God can do. I was not to set my mind on what I could see, but on what I could *not* see. Although I knew that Jennifer was in heaven,

24

the Lord gave me insight into eternal issues. They are the reality, not what we see with our eyes. During that dreaded time I knew Jennifer was just as she had always been: loving, caring, innocent, happy, and in the Lord's delightful presence. I was also aware of angels which surround our entry to heaven and which, though unseen, are always our companions. I felt the nearness of heaven and, for that, I thanked my loving Father. I thanked him too for the fortitude and bearing up of Andrew and our two young boys.

Why does God call our afflictions, i.e. our sorrows, cares, sadnesses and worries, light things? They are anything but light to us, for we feel their weight crushing down upon us. God our Father weighs them out as grams compared to eternity's load of blessings and 'eternal glory that far outweighs them all' (2 Corinthians 4:17). Amazingly each of these afflictions works for us, as we keep our eyes fixed ahead as Jesus did: 'who, for the joy set before him endured the cross' (Hebrews 12:2).

Jesus draws near
But the following day I saw none of this. Finding myself alone I busied myself tidying up. It didn't work. I tried not to give in to tears as I saw and lifted all that had belonged to Jennifer. Finally, in the bathroom, with her own personal items, the awful finality of death hit me. Once the tears

started there was no holding back the violent suffocating sobs. I would never see her again. I wished that I, too, could die.

There are no situations in which God is unable to comfort. His title, 'The God of all comfort' (2 Corinthians 1:3), is a worthy one. Through my tears I called on his name for help ... but with the thought that even God could not help me now. 'Dear Father, please help me. I know you will not bring her back. Let me die too so that I can go to her.' There followed another stream of bitter tears as I picked up *Daily Light*. I could read nothing. My tears were unwipable as well as unstoppable. Twice I tried to read ... but I could not. The third time I read these words more clearly, 'And God shall wipe away all tears from their eyes; and there shall be no more death, neither sorrow nor crying ... for the former things are passed away' (Revelation 21:4, AV). The whole page was on this theme, ending with 'The things which are not seen are eternal' (2 Corinthians 4:18, AV). As I thought upon these wonderful words, even though eternity seemed so far away, I was conscious of the presence of the Lord Jesus, so intimate, so near, as one who wept with me. I was learning how our Saviour is touched with all our weaknesses, and therefore is wonderfully able to comfort and strengthen. 'In all their distress he too was distressed' (Isaiah 63:9).

Mark and Philip were soon back at school.

Philip started a new school, one to which Jennifer was also due to go. Andrew was back at work. No-one had any heart in anything. We still had many visitors, and how grateful we were for every one of them. After a few weeks the time came for something we both dreaded. Andrew was to come home after the children had gone to school, and we would begin to sort out all Jennifer's things. We had decided to give most of them to a local children's home. I came back that morning wondering how I could do it, it seemed like giving her away. As I waited for Andrew I took myself to prayer – to the bathroom again. As on so many other occasions I wept as I prayed, feeling that I could part with nothing. We had already discussed this, Andrew and I, wanting no shrines, those never-to-be-forgotten places and never-to-be-touched things of happier times. Jennifer was with the Lord. The trouble was I wanted her here with me.

A lesson in love

As I tried to pray I was arrested with a clear question: 'Pat, do you love me?' Like Peter of old I quickly affirmed the Lord of my love to him. Then I realised just how weak my love really was, for although the Lord had Jennifer I didn't want to let her go. As I began thinking about this, into my heart came the words: 'For God so loved the world, that he gave his only begotten Son, that whosoever believeth in him should not perish, but have everlasting life' (John 3:16, AV). I had avowed my love to God. Now he showed me what love was all about. His love to me, the greatness of which can never be known nor adequately portrayed, moved his own heart to give his beloved Son for me. And didn't this mean leaving glory to come into a sin-darkened world to die on a cruel cross? .... For me? For the first time I saw something of what it must have cost him to send his dear Son, his only Son, for sinners like me. How much easier then to give my daughter back from a place such as this into the hands and immediate presence of the One who had so loved us. The tears flowed, but for a very different reason.

To block God out at such times and undertake a DIY job of heart mending just doesn't work. We are neither skilled nor qualified for the job. God is. 'The Spirit of the Sovereign Lord is on me... He has sent me to bind up the broken-hearted ... to comfort all who mourn, and provide for those who grieve in Zion' (Isaiah 61:1-3). It is his work. Why then did I begin to think that his help would not always be available? Surely God would not want to help me in these wonderful ways all the time? Perhaps I should try to stand on my own two feet. Such was my thinking some time later. And so it was, on one particular occasion, when I thought I could 'go it alone' my world fell in! But I determined to see it through. I can be obstinate; perhaps proud would be more truthful. I did get through, but in a slimy, muddy kind of way. There was certainly nothing in it for which to praise God.

Comforting and comforted

One evening some time later, when Philip was having a shower, I wondered why he was taking so long. Calling to him to open the door I found him in such a sorrowful state. On trying to comfort him he would have none of it, telling me that it was not tears but only the water from the shower running down his face and that he was fine! Philip will never know how grieved I felt, and how my heart went out to him. No, I could not bring Jennifer back, but I could comfort him. I could not make the world a better place, but I could share in his sorrow – and how I longed to. Every mother knows that when her child is hurt she feels the hurt more intensely. Mothers are like that.

Soon after that incident I read these words: 'Jacob tore his clothes, put on sackcloth and mourned for his son many days. All his sons and daughters came to comfort him, but he refused to be comforted' (Genesis 37:34-35). God had given me an object lesson – never refuse his comfort! I learned then that God is intensely moved by all that touches us, and that he yearns with a loving Father's heart to succour and uphold us, being grieved when we shun his comfort with our unbelief. We ought never to be like Jacob, refusing to be comforted. I found this wonderful truth a strength on many future occasions. The lovely fact is that Jesus ministers to our need, whatever our need might be. There have been many 'if onlys', which grief and tragedy always bring, but God has lovingly smoothed and smothered each one with new realisations of his Lordship in every area of our lives. Throughout all these years, and to this very day, he has sustained us, often in very difficult times.

At the time of writing, no-one has been charged or convicted of Jennifer's murder. But we know God has not forgotten us. Whether he does this or not is totally in his control and in his own time. And what of bitterness? Has that reared its callous head with all its blame and recrimination against God? I can only say very humbly that it has not. The love of my Father God has both overwhelmed me and upheld me and I have needed no explanation from him whose ways and will are perfect. Andrew rejoices as well, for he too is now saved, and committed to the Lord. We are also the proud grandparents of two lovely grandchildren.

One thing is sure – heaven lies ahead, the answers will be apparent, and a great reunion enjoyed.

2

ELIZABETH AND DONALD MACKAY

Elizabeth begins their story

'You've had your life, but what about me? Look at me. I haven't had time to do anything yet.' The speaker was a young girl, the age of one of our children. She has MS and is much more disabled than I am. She believes that a cruel fate, whom she calls God, has caused her illness and she has very little hope. How privileged I am! In the last few years God has helped me so much. Some have asked, 'Don't you ever ask "Why me?"' In the light of my friend's question, one might ask, 'Why not me?' So many people have problems. I have had a good life, and thank God for a Christian home. A happy marriage followed a happy childhood. Donald and I have been blessed with three children, good health in the main, and many good friends. Above all, we have had a sense of God's love and provision.

By my secondary school years I was learning that God uses his word, the Bible, to help and encourage his children. I still can picture the eve of my Higher English exam, the most important exam in my school career so far. I felt I knew nothing and was in a real panic. It seemed as if the months of preparation had gone for nothing. In despair I put my books away and prepared for bed. As usual I picked up my Bible. I don't remember what I read, but across the middle of my Scripture Union notes was written: 'Hitherto hath the Lord helped us' (1 Samuel 7:12, AV). These words cleared my brain and restored my powers of thought. I could see that this text was absolutely true. God had helped me all the way and he would not let me down now. God kept his word. At the end of my university career the same words presented themselves the evening before my finals.

The years passed and the time for our wedding drew near. We looked at one unsuitable house after another. Then, two months before we were married in 1965, the same words appeared again, framed on a bedroom wall of the house that was to be our home for the next ten years. Time and again these words have reassured me of God's wise provision and have renewed flagging faith. Was it coincidence I was reading in 1 Samuel when I was in hospital undergoing tests which revealed the nature of my illness?

My story so far, by Donald
Like Elizabeth, I had been brought up in a Christian family, but my experience of coming to

faith was not as untroubled as hers. It took a crisis during my student days to show me that I could not run my life alone. It was a great relief to roll all my burdens on to someone stronger and more loving than I could have believed possible, and to start to live life to his glory. A civil service career opened up, offering varied experiences, and opportunities to prove God's faithfulness. Marriage (at the advanced age of 35!) and a family were further blessings.

When I retired in 1988 we may have had momentary fears of my becoming a tedious house-husband, always getting in the way of the real job of running a home. It was partly for that reason that I embarked on a theological course. For three sessions this occupied me happily during the mornings. Elizabeth meantime kept active, chairing an Abbeyfield home, supervising an outreach café during the Edinburgh Festival, looking after her mother, and keeping up a wide correspondence. Our three children had left home but were not infrequent visitors.

How the problem began – Elizabeth explains
In 1990 I received an invitation to a birthday party. The party was in Germany, and the invitation came from a friend whom I have known since 1957. Our friendship was deep and it was a joy to spend time together. While I was there, I had indications that all was not well with my health.

33

For months the words 'Do not be afraid' had been occurring frequently in my daily Bible readings. Once it had been: 'Do not be afraid, you are not going to die' (Judges 6:23). Their frequency and the effect they seemed to be having made me remark to my husband, 'I wonder if God is trying to tell me something?' I had an X-ray examination. By the time I returned to hospital for results, things had returned to normal. Perfectly normal X-ray pictures received little attention. Instead I found myself asked to do all sorts of queer things. I felt like a performing poodle. Scarcely had I time to draw breath before I was called back to spend a week in Edinburgh Royal Infirmary.

The night before admission I felt rather apprehensive, guessing that I was facing something serious. As a Christian, I had secretly wondered how I would cope with real difficulties. I read *Daily Light*, the book containing short related texts on a given theme. What I read made me turn to my Bible. I read how Jesus was the true vine, we the branches, and God the Father the gardener. To make branches more fruitful he prunes them. This made sense. I had seen a pruned vine once. The comparison with someone with severe MS, which was what I began to suspect might be the problem, was fair. Another verse led me to 2 Corinthians 1. We are able to comfort, as Christ has comforted us. I read on. Paul, the writer, had suffered an illness where he despaired of life, but

God delivered him and would deliver him from his present trials. The Corinthians were urged to help by their prayers. I felt this promise of deliverance was for me.

With such explanation of the reason for my illness, as far as I was concerned; its purpose for others; and its final outcome, I felt able to face anything. I had once before, when facing surgery, been the subject of much prayer, it was almost palpable. I knew God would answer prayer, whether in time or eternity I did not know, but I trusted it would be in this life. God does not promise everything will be easy, but he does promise his presence.

If God had encouraged me the evening before, my morning reading – the end of the story of Ruth – was even more wonderful. The previous day I read how Ruth's world had collapsed with the death of her husband. Her husband's brother and father had died and her mother-in-law whom she loved was going away. Ruth did not want to go back to her old life. She was determined to go with her mother-in-law. I read of her setting out on an apparently hopeless journey and how her life was subsequently transformed. She did not realise it, but she was to become, humanly speaking, the ancestress of God's Son, the Messiah. My Bible Study notes pointed out how God had used apparent human disasters in wonderful ways. 'And we know that in all things God works for the good of those who love him' (Romans 8:28). I trusted that that included us.

Donald takes up the story

The diagnosis of MS made no great impact on our family life. We saw no point in peering into the future. Elizabeth, after all, had already had an alarming incident eight years before, requiring hospitalization and a whole battery of tests. The condition had been diagnosed as *diabetes insipidus* (this is quite different from sugar diabetes) and was fairly easily controlled. For MS we knew that there was no treatment, but that in many older folk the disability progressed slowly, sometimes with episodes of remission. A course of steroids produced a marked improvement in her balance and control.

The doctors remained puzzled, however, over some aspects of Elizabeth's symptoms, and following further tests they decided that the more probable diagnosis was degeneration of the cerebellum, which is the part of the brain responsible for semiautomatic functions and through which all the nerve messages to and from the brain have to pass. This meant a different outlook, a slow but steady deterioration, with no remissions but perhaps some 'plateaux'. I rebelled. What were the chances of Elizabeth having two rare and unconnected conditions? Was it not more likely that her present problems were due to some complication arising from the *diabetes insipidus*? A second opinion was obtained, but after a further scan they told us that they were now pretty sure that the cerebellar explanation was correct. We should accept the fact and adjust to it.

'A command or a promise?' asks Elizabeth

I remembered from my old SU card that we were encouraged, when reading Scripture, to ask ourselves, 'Is there a command to obey or a promise to claim?' James 5:14 contains both a command and a promise: 'Is any one of you sick? He should call the elders of the church to pray over him ... and the prayer offered in faith will make the sick person well ...' We did just that. There was no immediate cure, although my handwriting improved for a time. God seemed to be saying, 'I have heard, I am in control, trust me.' I realised the need for patience. One great benefit of the elders coming for prayer was the assurance we were given that prayer would continue. We were also assured that if we needed help, that help would be given – at any hour of day or night. What an encouraging example of Christian love.

Donald fills in the facts

Nearly two years had now passed and Elizabeth had lost quite a lot of ground. She could still walk and drive a car, but was losing strength in her left leg, and coordination of movement was becoming harder. Eventually the time came when the GP recommended applying for an orange disabled badge. Next came a wheelchair – just for occasional use, but quite soon a necessity.

Holidays ... Elizabeth makes arrangements

God promises that he will withhold no good thing from those who love him. We now had an example of that. Janet and Finlay, our daughter and son-in-law, had decided to go on holiday to Austria. They knew Donald would enjoy the trip, but were afraid to suggest he join them in case I would feel I was missing out. Having heard indirectly of their plans I decided to make other arrangements so that Donald could go. Friends invited me for a holiday with them. It suited my needs and I enjoyed it thoroughly. It gave the others even greater enjoyment in their expedition.

The problems as Donald saw them

For me, things were closing in. After my theological course, I felt able to take on further study on environmental matters, in which I had played a part during my working life. As a postgraduate student of Aberdeen University, I found it practicable to work at home, with visits to libraries in Edinburgh and the occasional trip to Aberdeen. It was a race against time to complete my thesis while Elizabeth was able to cope on her own, but we made it. The graduation took place in November 1994, with our son Colin being capped at the same time, and four stalwart student volunteers whisking the wheelchair effortlessly up the enormous flight of stairs to the Mitchell Hall.

Talking of stairs, we had to decide whether to move our bedroom to the ground floor. Elizabeth had been struggling upstairs with increasing difficulty. The social services came up with a very generous solution. A ground floor shower/toilet was installed free of charge, while a stairlift was heavily subsidised. Although the stairlift was not installed for several months, either Colin or Alasdair was able to be at home every night to help carry their mother upstairs. God may not deal with problems by removing them, but by making coping possible. Problems there certainly have been in increasing measure. Elizabeth's eyesight has deteriorated, so that the eye cannot fix for long on, for example, a line of print. Her consultant issued a certificate of visual impairment. This means that she has access to Talking Books and the extensive tape library of the Torch Trust.

She no longer has the strength to move a wheelchair manually – as the orthopaedic specialist put it somewhat crudely: 'You really have the use of only one limb out of four.' However, an electric wheelchair, which is very manoeuvrable, gives Elizabeth the free run of the ground floor. A ramp at the back door allows access to the garden.

Being tied to a wheelchair, however, means that blood circulation is slow and legs and feet get very cold, even in summer. The health service has an answer to that problem as well. Electric socks have been supplied, giving a gentle heat which is a great comfort, in the evenings especially. There is even a battery supplied which allows Elizabeth to move about in her chair for a short period.

'What of the future?' asks Elizabeth

What of the future? I know that I am still losing ground. There have been things which, had I been able to anticipate them, would have made me afraid, but in fact we have been able to cope. On the other hand we have had the privilege of seeing how God has used my condition as a means of blessing to others. As someone who has become a friend as the direct result of my illness reminded me: 'If answered prayers are just coincidences, why is it that, when I stop praying, the coincidences stop happening?' It is a blessing to experience God's faithfulness and to know that he is in control.

Needing support and being supported – Donald explains

How has all this impacted on me? Physically, I have been able to cope with the steadily increasing demands of lifting. In case the effort becomes too great in the course of time, the occupational therapist has plans for some form of lifting device to help me.

Much the greater problem is the mental one. To witness a loved one losing ground is not easy. I am thankful that the process has been gradual, making it possible for both of us to adjust to new situations and relationships. Of course, it makes a huge difference that Elizabeth is so strong in her mind and spirit, always trying to look positively at the challenges confronting her and to turn them to good use.

It would be idle to pretend that everything has been positive. There have been strains and stresses, and times of gloom and self-pity on both sides. I had a brief episode of clinical depression, relieved by pills and exercise. The social services have now arranged nursing and home help visits to allow me the best part of a day off per week. There is also a respite care arrangement at Liberton Hospital every two months or so which Elizabeth has used creatively. Neither can we overestimate the privilege of belonging to a church fellowship. Buccleuch and Greyfriars Free Church has been our spiritual home throughout our married life, and never has its value been more apparent than now. Again and again the word expounded during Sunday services has proved exactly what we needed at the time. We know of so many who are praying regularly for us, and there must be many others, in the congregation and throughout the wider denomination, whom we do not know. Practical help comes in varied forms, and often before we have recognised the need for it ourselves.

If we keep a grip on the fact that he is the one who has brought us where we are, that he works all things for good to those who love him, and that he himself is with and beside us in the deep waters, then we have the key to all that lies ahead.

'No easy answers,' concludes Elizabeth

Have I changed? As time has progressed almost every sense has been adversely affected. Sight, hearing, touch, the ability to move, even to turn over in bed, speech, so that it becomes an effort to carry on a conversation – it would be boring to list every problem. I am grateful there has been no real change of personality or loss of mental faculties.

As physical ability has changed, so there has had to be a change in life style. Instead of being a carer, I am the one being cared for. Instead of being at the centre of activities, I am very much on the periphery or excluded. But many other people as the result of accident, age or illness find themselves in a similar situation, perhaps with no one willing or able to help. One no longer has ordinary human contacts in shops, buses or simply in the street. The privilege of Sunday worship becomes doubly precious. So too is any visit, however brief.

Every situation has two sides. I have chosen to list the problems one might expect to be part of such an illness as I have. Viewed from a different angle, as a Christian, I have already been assured that God is in control, and I have experienced the privilege of being shown in advance what God was doing.

I have often thought about the reasons I believe God gave me for this illness. Pruning, for fruitfulness, I had thought of in my relationship with others. Recently I saw an uncared-for rose bed. Apart from a blanket of weeds, the roses had not been pruned, perhaps for several years, and how pitiful they were. I realised that the Master Gardener knew how to prune plants to make them strong and shapely. He wanted them to fulfil the purpose he had for them when he planted them. The fruit of the Spirit is love, joy, peace, patience, kindness, goodness, faithfulness, gentleness and self-control (Galatians 5:22).

Without God's intervention, left to ourselves we are more likely to be like that neglected rose bed.

Reading and writing

In several books recently I have met the thought: 'Be careful when you ask God to make you more useful to him, he may take you at your word.' God's dealing with us may not be particularly comfortable. All that is unsatisfactory has to be dealt with. My task, then, must be to comfort others as Christ has comforted me. In my own strength how miserably I fail. We so desperately need God's grace. When Paul prayed that his health problem might be taken away, God answered, 'My grace is sufficient for you, for my power is made perfect in weakness' (2 Corinthians 12:9). How often has that verse helped me.

I have no great literary claims. An article, written to show how God had helped me by his word, was published in *Life and Work*, a magazine that has a fairly wide circulation. Thanks to the editor's skill, it was presented effectively. One lady known to us was terminally ill, and about to go into a hospice for the last days of her life. A mutual friend brought her a copy of the article. She read and re-read it, and then would not let it out of her sight. I imagine that the title of the article, 'Do not be afraid', which had been supplied by the editor, was just what she needed. Some days later, shortly before she died, I referred to 'the peace of God which passeth all understanding' (Philippians 4:7, AV). Her smile conveyed her agreement.

Perhaps my one activity useful to other people is my letter writing. It may be that God uses these letters. It is hard to judge such things.

Having seen how God has confirmed that I had correctly interpreted two of the Bible readings which I was given on the evening before I went into hospital to have my condition investigated, I can trust in the deliverance he assured me of. I once remarked to an old friend, 'I don't know if this deliverance will be in time or eternity.' 'Both,' was his prompt reply.

At present it would be dishonest to refuse to admit that life is difficult. Donald has to do everything while I can do nothing practically to help. It is a blow to one's pride to see how things go on without one. The past few years have brought a veritable army of professional helpers. Even if one does not always agree with the way they set about things, the least one can do is to show how greatly they are appreciated.

It is obvious that my former activities are no longer possible. But nowhere in the Bible are we discharged from serving God because of illness. A local hospital offers respite care. There, the staff are dedicated and helpful. Many patients are more disabled than I am. Many have little hope. Is this where God wants me to be? Faith is often respected without being shared. People are quick to notice inconsistency. How important to refrain from critical attitudes and from preaching at people. It has become clear that my eyes should be on Jesus, not on others to criticise them.

How can I answer my young friend? There are no easy answers. As a child, I remember singing, 'Anywhere with Jesus I can safely go.' Now, half a century later, I am more convinced than ever that he is the answer and that I can safely go into the future, whatever it holds, hand in hand with him.

3

JOHN MEIKLEJOHN

The head that emerged from the hatch on the deck of the minesweeper alongside the quay closely resembled my idea of Rob Roy McGregor or some other wild Highlander. It was crowned with a mop of ginger hair and surrounded by a forest of ginger whiskers. The stoker from the tug I was about to join nudged me. 'See him,' he said, 'he's mad, he preaches on street corners.' I thought, 'Lord, so soon?', swallowed, and said, 'So do I.'

It was 1955. I was a year out of the Royal Navy and had spent that year as an engineer on one of Her Majesty's salvage vessels. From being converted at the age of 15 I had slowly drifted and had reached the stage of making a bargain with God. 'Lord,' I said, 'if you get me away from this mess I'm in, I'll witness for you and serve you.' A transfer from the Clyde to Sheerness Dockyard in Kent followed, and it was on my first day in Sheerness that God expected me to fulfil my side of the bargain. Looking back, God's plan can be seen clearly, but then it was a step of faith which proved to be the first of many in a satisfying walk with God.

During my first year at Sheerness I married

Irene, and at the end of that year we faced our first hurdle together when the dockyard closed and redundancy threatened. A move to working as a Port Missionary in Scotland followed. Initially satisfying, it proved burdensome in the end. Desperate and unhappy, I applied for job after job before being accepted as a Welfare and After Care Officer in the Scottish Prison Service.

Sound advice

I have never forgotten the advice given to me by my boss during the first week. 'Mr Meiklejohn,' he said, 'you will be dealing with dishonest people, people who are liars, thieves and cheats. You must deal with them with total honesty otherwise you will lose your credibility and their trust and respect.'

I have been 'conned' by the very best – the elite of the trade. George C told me a tale which had me convinced he was genuine, repentant and in need, and that I was the only one in the world who could help him. I did, and soon realised I had been 'conned'. On many occasions I have listened to similar tales told with equal pathos and expertise, responding that I had been conned by the very best and recognised amateurs. Very often the reply was a grin and, 'I had to try'.

Early in my career I met the lifers, many of them having had a death sentence commuted and life imprisonment substituted. As I might one day be involved with someone awaiting execution I had to decide where I stood regarding the state taking a life as decreed by law. Indeed, when I went to work at Aberdeen Prison, one of the prisoners with whom I was involved told me that there was nothing wrong with him that six feet of hemp couldn't have cured some time earlier.

Believing, as I did, that I was in the Prison Service because God wanted me there, I concluded that since God had placed me in the Service at a time when capital punishment was still on the statute books, that, if the occasion ever arose, I should do whatever was demanded of me. I had for my guidance: 'Submit yourselves for the Lord's sake to every authority instituted among men: whether to the king, as the supreme authority, or to governors, who are sent by him to punish those who do wrong ...' (1 Peter 2:13-14). I was involved only once with a condemned man, the last to be executed in Scotland, and I worked with him and his family, assisting in arranging some of his final visits before the execution took place. I was not sorry when capital punishment was removed from the statute books.

From time to time I have been asked, 'How can you work with people who have committed such evil acts?' I did not regard them like that, but as people who had the same problems as the rest of us. I saw them as who they were, rather than what they had done. It was necessary for security purposes to consider the nature of the offence and the length of sentence imposed, but beyond that I tried to treat prisoners as persons in their own right. Not only did that offer individuality and dignity, it also helped remove emotive response in decision making when dealing with people serving similar sentences but who had committed their offences in passion or with cold premeditation. There were difficult times because some people can only be described as evil. With them it is not easy to be dispassionate.

We'll meet again

Prison staff are mobile, and I have worked in ten different prisons throughout Scotland and lived in nine different houses. Moving house is one of the most stressful events in one's life. Children have to change schools and make new friends, or, should the move come at a critical time in their education, be left behind in the care of friends or family. There is also the Christian priority of finding a new church. Moving can also be a blessing, for we now have friends throughout Scotland.

Prisoners move too. Because some transfer from prison to prison as they progress through their sentences, and others serve further sentences in different jails, staff meet up with the same people over and over again. James was among the first of the lifers I came across. We met in Aberdeen. Fifteen years later, in another prison, he was delighted to see me. I was a familiar face, a continuity in his life, as was my Chief Officer. James could remember when Chief T was a young officer at Barlinnie. It is sad when the main events of a man's life are so closely related to time spent in custody.

Because of changes in the Service I had to decide if I wanted to remain in the Prison Service or become a Probation Officer. Both required further training, but at that time Assistant Governors were needed. I applied and was accepted. I had eight months at College in Wakefield, followed by a posting to Polmont Borstal. It was there I realised the full extent of the work done by Christian volunteers who operated Bible Classes at the invitation of the Chaplains. The work goes on today, often in association with Prison Fellowship. I know of many who have been reached for Christ through the faithful work of Christians called by God to serve in Bible Classes within prisons and Young Offender's Institutions.

Having begun my career as a Governor, I knew that my Christian faith had to direct how I carried out my duties and be seen in action in my life. I had to be an open letter for Jesus, or, as Paul put it: 'You show that you are a letter from Christ' (2 Corinthians 3:3). My duties and how I did them had to glorify Almighty God. An open witness and testimony to staff and inmates was respected and it allowed for any who wanted to make a personal approach, which was usually prefaced by, 'You're a Christian, aren't you?'

Colourful characters – on both sides of the bars
I enjoyed working with 'characters'. They added colour to life and, by the force of their personalities, stood out and were noticed. Rev Sandy was one of my favourites. He was a part time chaplain who looked like a farmer. Gruff, sometimes abrupt, he could always be relied on to go the extra mile. When he saw a need he went all out to help.

One of my immediate bosses was another character. He decided the role he was expected to play and played it with all the skill and enthusiasm of a thespian. When discipline was called for he was a disciplinarian; when investigation was required he investigated with all the enthusiasm of Sherlock Holmes. It was from him I learned that even if a man was in prison he still deserved respect and dignity from those in authority over him.

'Sammy' was a rogue, a likeable rogue who had an eye for the opportune moment, and who took constant risks to better the authorities. He manipulated the system skilfully and with aplomb, accepting what came when he was caught as his just desserts. Sammy was an up front character with a hard shell beyond which few men reached. I had to send for him to tell him that his father, his only relative, had died. He sat and wept great tears of grief, dried them off, rose from his chair and said, 'Thanks for telling me on my own, Boss, it's our secret.' The next day he was the same old Sammy presenting his facade to the world.

Sammy, now dead, reminded me that Jesus sees us as we are and not as we appear.

Real life drama

A lifer taught me another lesson. He clothed himself in a cloak of silence, speaking only when absolutely necessary. Living in his silent world, he seemed immune to the vagaries of prison life. We started a drama group at the prison, and presented a one act play. It had gone well, and the men who wanted to be more adventurous were preparing for the performance of a three act play. The Governor was the producer and I was involved in back stage work. One night, to our surprise, the silent lifer was in the group. He sat away on his own, communicated with no one, but watched everything. This went on for a few weeks and he was accepted as just 'being there'.

Rehearsals were well under way and we were preparing the off stage effects. The effects men had to produce a loud bang using a theatrical firework and flashing lights. Everything was in place but we were having problems getting our cue for pressing the switch. At the fourth or fifth wrong timing I was gently pushed aside, and a voice in my ear said, 'Get out the road.' Our silent lifer pushed past me to take my place at the switch. The lines were spoken, the cue came, and with perfect timing he threw the switch. He kept his place in the crew and, although never becoming a brilliant conversationalist, he did talk from that time on. Our new effects man taught me never to give up hope, even when things seem hopeless.

There is a 'grapevine' among prisoners by which news spreads with remarkable speed. What came as a surprise was that it also dealt in prophecy. I had been called to a promotion board and the results usually took about a fortnight to come through, with the posting for successful candidates coming around a month later. Some ten days after I had been to the board Sammy greeted me with, 'Young fella, you've been promoted and you're going to Glenochil.' I asked if he had a hot line to the Scottish Office! A few days later my promotion was confirmed, as was my posting to Glenochil. I still haven't worked that one out.

My stay at Glenochil was brief. Only nine months after arriving I was told I was being posted to Dumfries to take charge of the Young Offender's Institution there. We were shattered by the news. It meant that one of our sons would be going to his third secondary school in three years, and that my wife, who had gone back to district nursing, would have to give up her job. We spent a lot of time as a family talking this through, and Irene and I were much in prayer to God about it. Our eldest son had been left behind in lodgings in Perth to finish his schooling, and he had already made comments about having no settled home. A further move would upset the others. It seemed best that I should live in the Dumfries Governor's house alone, being joined by the family at weekends.

Househunting and heartsearching

We went house hunting for Irene and the family, eventually submitting an offer for a property. The few days we spent awaiting the response must have been among the blackest of our experience. We both felt foreboding. There seemed to be a darkness over, and a heaviness within, that neither of us could shrug off. The night before we were due to hear if our offer had been accepted, Irene lay awake. Describing her thoughts later, she said, 'It was as if I was planning a divorce. I lay thinking of what would go to Dumfries and what would stay in Alva. And the more I thought of it, the more distressed I became.' It was a battle – a battle within our minds and a battle in our spirits. Our constant prayer was that God would overrule anything not in his plan for us, and that he would do his will with us.

Midway through the following morning the lawyer telephoned. Our offer had been refused. We accepted that as God's answer immediately. Apparently the seller had turned it down without consulting his wife or his lawyer, both of whom subsequently asked us to resubmit the offer with the assurance it would be accepted. But for us the cloud had lifted. God had answered our prayers.

He wanted us in Dumfries as a family and we obeyed willingly. It was just as well. My term at Glenochil was eleven months, but I was to be at Dumfries for nine years.

Whenever Dumfries made the media headlines it was described as 'Scotland's Toughest Young Offender's Institution'. In many ways it both earned and deserved that title. It held about a hundred and twenty young men between the ages of sixteen and twenty one, and all were serving sentences of three years or more. When I went there as Governor about forty were serving sentences of life, or what was termed Her Majesty's Pleasure, which was an indeterminate sentence akin to life for someone under the age of eighteen when sentenced. There were some who just wanted to get on with their sentences, some who were determined to challenge authority head on, and others who sat back, watched, assessed, and moved to suit themselves when they decided the time was right. There were lads who were gang members; bookmakers and their followers; bullies and those who were bullied: a hotch potch of teenage temperaments. It was the job of the staff to keep a lid on it all in such a way as to enable each young man in the place to live his life peacefully and safely.

The bullies were always a problem, particularly when they directed their attention to boys convicted of crimes against women or children.

It was as a result of dealing with a lad planning vengeance on those who were bullying him that I met with Fred Lemon, who was converted while a convict in Dartmoor Prison. Jerry had been at the receiving end of threats and planned revenge on a grand scale by plotting gang warfare. The intelligence system in the prison kept us abreast of what was happening and, eventually, I decided it would be better for all concerned, particularly Jerry, if he were to be removed from circulation for a while. He was quietly lodged in a separate cell and kept out of contact with his cronies who, without their leader, dispersed. Jerry, with nothing better to do, started to work his way through some library books. One of them was *Breakout* by Fred Lemon. As his books had impressed me greatly I had put them in the library. One day Jerry mentioned that he had written to Mr Lemon and he was coming to visit him. As a result Fred and I struck up a delightful friendship. I'm still grateful to Jerry.

The Bible Class at Dumfries was a vital part of life there. It was not unusual to have fifty young men attending, and a valuable spiritual work was done. How well I remember the night I received a call from Jimmy McD to tell me that he had led one of the young men to the Lord. It was a true conversion, and J C still keeps in touch.

Cinderella with style

The Orderly Room was held each day at 10.30am. It was there that requests were made and answered, and also where the Institution discipline was administered. One of the toughest of the young men came to the Orderly Room and asked if it was true that I had been involved in a Drama Group at Perth. The follow-up was a Drama Group in Dumfries and a pantomime at Christmas. The Group started with as big a bunch of villains as ever professed interest in the dramatic arts. My offer to get them a script was refused with disdain and they wrote their own. *Cinderella* in rough verse resulted, and I was glad I had reserved the right of editing and censorship. The two ugly sisters were the biggest and brawniest in the group. No make up was required.

The first night came and the audience was made up of all the other lads from the Institution. In a tense atmosphere the heckling and barracking started even before curtain rise. The reception of Cinderella, a good-looking lad in drag, was good for some noise. But when the ugly sisters arrived in dresses, high heels, handbags and lipstick, pandemonium broke loose. The actors continued valiantly, but no one could hear them. We were seriously considering stopping the show. There was no need. The bigger ugly sister, never breaking off his lines, stepped down from the low stage, belted the nearest bloke with his handbag, laid him flat on his back, and got back on stage still speaking. The audience settled down and enjoyed the show.

The Orderly Room was where I heard one of the most delightful requests of my career. We had been required to change from being a Young Offender's Institution to being a Prison. While altering the population and age range, we retained what was best in our programme, including the Bible Class. Some months later a man came with a request to start a prayer meeting. I was delighted and told him so. He said that six or seven men wanted to meet in the Chaplain's Room on Thursdays at 7pm. When I asked about the day and the timing I was told, 'Thursday at 7 is *Top of the Pops*, so that means if they come to the prayer meeting it's because they mean it.' His devastating logic made me wonder what I was prepared to sacrifice for a prayer meeting.

After nine years at Dumfries I was promoted and transferred to Cornton Vale, the only prison in Scotland for women. I found adapting from an all male situation to one which was predominantly female quite strange. Discipline was easier, and it seemed odd to see prisoners walking unescorted to their work. I was bewildered to find myself in a world where PMT was an accepted problem and even an excuse. There were times at Cornton Vale when I felt ashamed of being a man. So many of the women and girls who came to us were victims of men. They had been abused, and bore the scars in their personalities. Many had no perception of their own value, and some resorted to self mutilation. I was saddened by that, and also by the fact that despite the work done by the Chaplain and the Deaconess, very few of the women showed any interest in spiritual matters.

Cornton Vale was perhaps the happiest time of my service. The staff were keen, thinking carefully about what they were doing and really caring for their charges. Quite a number were Christians, and it showed. All of them, regardless of their faith or lack of it, constantly reminded me of the need to show care and concern for the people around us.

It was God who put me in the Prison Service, and it was he who gave me the ability and wisdom to cope. Mountains of difficulty there were, but they could be removed. Trials were as real as God's presence in them. And times of delight were shared with him.

4

KAY REID

'I've decided to go to Edinburgh and try to find work there.'

'Will the children and I come with you or shall we come up when you have found something?'

'I am going alone. This is the end of "us". I won't fight you for the children. I don't want anything from the house except my clothes and a few personal belongings. The tenancy of the house will be put in your name and I will leave as soon as possible.'

As I swung around to confirm what I was hearing, our children arrived home from church with a friend. With good-natured teasing and raucous laughter they spent the evening looking through photograph albums, including our wedding album. My husband joined in, pointing out funny pictures and telling stories about the photographs in front of them. My mind raced from our conversation to this family scene, and over incidents spanning the past ten years.

'All over! All over! What am I going to do?' I wanted to scream at them to be quiet and let me think. But I smiled, made coffee and tea, and washed the dishes.

I had been to church and Sunday School as long as I could remember. My father took us to church and my mother stayed at home. Neither were Christians, but they did think it was the right thing to do to take children to church. From the age of four I was aware that God had something special for me to do. I wanted to find him, but no-one could tell me how or where. In 1960 I went to a Youth for Christ rally and heard that I could know God, I could be part of his family, I could have a real relationship with him! After the meeting I went forward and asked the young people to tell me how to know God. One girl sat down with me and showed me from the Bible that if I asked God into my life – received him – he would come in and live with me, he would forgive my sins and make me his child. Praying a very simple prayer I asked Jesus to forgive me and told him I wanted to give my life to him. I invited him to come and live in me, to change me. I was 12 years old. Never have I doubted that I am his child. He has guided me, helped me and been my constant companion and friend. I have had, and still have, a wonderful relationship with him.

Marriage ... the heights and the depths

In 1972 I married a lovely man. He was considerate, warm, compassionate, loved the Lord and wanted to serve him. I often thanked God for this man and for the love we had for each other. We were blessed with four children: three boys and one girl. Having struggled to find work in our area we moved down south where we lived for a number of years. During our time there my husband and I did a six month long Discipleship Training Course and a Leadership Training Course with our church. We were involved in the children's ministry, a Christian school, counselling and home fellowships. Two foster children were placed in our care for six and a half years and two more for six months. Many teenagers came to us for help and often lived with us for a while until they were able to cope. Our lives were full, exciting and fun. God blessed us and we often saw his wonderful provision and support. Sometimes my husband and I would find a kindly 'babysitter' and slip away for a weekend together. We seemed to have an enviable marriage.

Ten years later, in 1982, when our children were aged 9, 7, 6 and 4, I found out that my husband was having an affair with the daughter of a friend of ours. My life crashed in pieces around me. I was ashamed that he had betrayed his wife, his family and our friends. Sick and trembling I went to the Lord. At first I couldn't even pray or read my Bible. I just sat and cried. Then prayers that are etched on my memory poured out. 'Father, I don't know what to say. You know all about it. You can see my heart. I want to kill him. I want to hate him and hit him or the dog or the cat. Lord, that won't do any good, and will only make me sin. Oh God, help me to do the right thing. Help me to move in the opposite spirit to him. Don't let me react in the flesh but help me to be like you so that my children will not be damaged and our marriage saved.' Gradually the pain became numb and I saw the situation more rationally and objectively, rather like a nurse distancing herself from emotional involvement with a patient. My Christian friends and I confronted him about the affair.

With tears he protested his innocence and weakness to resist temptation. 'I couldn't help it. She seduced me!' Agreeing to go for counselling he apologised for his relationship with the young woman, insisting it would never happen again. I forgave him and attended counselling with him. Our marriage was so precious we both needed to do all we could to make things right, to sort out our lives and save the marriage, so glorifying God in our lives. We went to see the minister of our congregation and marriage counsellors.

One counsellor told me that I was a rebellious and unsubmissive wife and that there was sin in my life. That, I was told, was why everything was going wrong in our marriage. God was judging me for my attitude and hardness of heart.

Shocked, I repented of everything I could think of and pled for forgiveness. In my heart I couldn't believe that God had such a vindictive nature. I went back to all the teaching we had received at the Discipleship Training Course about the Father-heart of God, reading wonderful passages about God's love for me and his forgiveness and gentleness. Through my pain, I began to see what I meant to God – and that he was not some awful judgmental deity sitting with a sword ready to sweep it down on me and my loved ones for the smallest wrong.

The struggle to go on

I tried to please my husband and wooed him. So that I could have more time for him I gave up my work with children. Fasting and agonising before God, I pled with him to change me and make me a better wife for this man he had chosen for me. Our relationship seemed better than it had been for a while. Things were improving, praise God! Gradually I began to trust my husband again. 'Every marriage goes through hard times,' I re-assured myself.

While I was peeling onions one evening the following year, my little daughter told me about the things she had seen her daddy doing with another woman. She was confused and thought she was bad because Daddy had told her not to tell anyone, and here she was telling me. How thankful I was for those onions. They disguised the real tears I shed as my family laughed at my oniony watery eyes. Resolving to wait, I watched and listened, having read somewhere that it was better exercise to dig for facts than to jump to conclusions! I was going to do some exercise and see what, if anything, I could dig up.

Quiet investigation and watchfulness disclosed that he had a string of other 'loves' in his life, sometimes more than one at a time.

I was devastated! Subjectivity prevailed and swamped me with fears and guilt. Where had I gone wrong? Was I such a useless woman that I could not make this man happy? Who could I go to who would help and not pile condemnation on my head? This time I waited, and asked the Lord to lead me to someone who could really support and help me, and, if possible, help my husband too. I was introduced to a lovely, wise woman who had a lot of counselling experience. We grew to know each other and, when I felt I could trust her, I began to share my cares. She was totally accepting of me. I felt no judgement or condemnation from her. We prayed together a lot and she asked God to give her wisdom as she helped me look at my situation.

I read everything I could about problems in marriage. Again I tried to meet my husband's needs, make him happy, keep his relationship with the children strong and maintain a stable home for the eight children living within it. I read books about relationships and how to make them better. I learned new cooking techniques. I dieted, did exercises and dressed better. That was when he accused me of having an affair and slapped me, telling me that I had better get my act together and behave like a real wife and stop flirting with other men!

Desperation

It was then I realised that I was not to blame. I couldn't do any more to make him happy or to make our marriage work. Examining the Scriptures, I clung to the promises I found there, for I realised that by then I was so low I was almost trying to pay God to work for me. If I tithed more could I persuade God to bless? Or if I fasted would he see I meant business and bless us? One awful day I put my Bible on the floor, stood on it and cried, 'There, God, I am standing on the promises of God! I don't know how else to do it.' I wept.

On the surface I was an able and competent woman. I still laughed and ministered and taught in the school. The children, apart from my daughter, were unaware of my state or of their father's infidelity. Everything appeared to be normal and right as I learned to wear a mask and to act well. Inwardly, I was deeply ashamed of myself and my failure to have a successful marriage. Pained all the time, I found feelings of guilt quite overwhelming. My health started to fail and I became chronically ill. Sometimes I welcomed the physical pain because it was familiar, explicable, treatable and took my mind off the trauma inside. I could cry and people were sympathetic but without knowing the real reason for my tears.

My husband's family all lived in Scotland. When his mother died, he came back home after the funeral and announced that he wanted to go back to Scotland to be nearer his family. Selling our house and some of our furniture, we moved to central Scotland. It was difficult to get somewhere to live at first but we found a small house in which we lived on top of each other for a year. The children attended school and the search for work began.

With this new start, where no-one knew about our marriage problems, it felt promising. Hope grew in me that this time God would work a miracle, that this would be the break that would restore our marriage and bring my husband back into close fellowship with the Lord. It wasn't. He became abusive in all sorts of ways, all the while blaming me for 'forcing him' to abuse me. And he went to church only to fall out with the leadership because they would not let him have a leadership position, despite his obvious gifts and experience. Wise leadership! The children were confused about the church's attitude and their father's anger at the 'injustice'. Gradually they began to question things, but he did not like that and accused me of turning them against him.

Many times I asked God just to take him, to let him die. Despite his sinful lifestyle he was a Christian. If he died he would be happy, and we would be free. Never once did I think of divorce. I had made vows before God and the only way I could get out of the mess they had brought upon me was if God worked a miracle or my husband died. As I was convinced that my children would be his targets if I died, I always asked God to keep me going until they were independent and could be out of any danger.

A hope and a future

During this time I prayed that the Lord would show me how to regain my strength in him so that I could be physically, emotionally and spiritually well. Before we moved, I felt God gave me the promise of Jeremiah 29:11: 'For I know the plans I have for you,' declares the Lord, '... plans to give you a hope and a future.' I struggled to believe it. Lovingly, my Father gave me confirmation again and again. The same verse was sent to me by three different people from three different countries and arriving on the same day! A child told me she had been praying for me and that she had a verse to share with me. It was the same one. Hope began to grow in my barrenness.

A year later, in May 1991, we were offered a large house and accepted it with great delight! How we enjoyed the freedom and space it gave us. At the beginning of June my husband told me he was leaving!

The children, all teenagers now, were shocked to be told by him, quite dispassionately, what he had done, what his plans were, that he did not want them and that he was leaving to start a new life for himself. They were angry, hurt, confused and overwhelmed with shame that their wonderful, upright father was not what they thought him to be. And they felt terribly rejected. Moving into a flat, he left the children and me to lick our wounds and start the job of rebuilding our lives. Within a few months he was living with a girlfriend, and once our divorce was granted he married her.

'Guess what, Mum, you've heard of disposable hankies and disposable gloves and all that – well, now you are a disposable wife!' Shelving my hurt, I worked at stabilizing them and teaching them the principles of forgiveness and drawing close to their Heavenly Father. I walked for hours with one or another of these hurting young people, listening and loving, hugging and praying. They took their anger and frustration out on me, arguing, swearing and accusing me; then crying, holding me and asking that I forgive them. In time they developed a new relationship with their father and, one by one, without discussing it with anyone first, they spoke out their forgiveness to him.

I found myself struggling with things I had

never dreamed of. By changing the motor insurance into my name I lost twenty five years of non claims bonus! I had to pay a deposit for 'reconnection' on my telephone because I was a new customer, although I had paid the bills for years with my own cheques! I was asked for my ex-husband's address and approval when I tried to open an account in my name. Even though it was known at the school that I was divorced and had sole custody of the children, I had to insist they contact me when a problem arose instead of my ex-husband. And I was subjected to an embarrassing barrage of questions about my private life to get Income Support, and had to wade through the humiliating process of obtaining benefits which only last for a short while before the whole business starts again.

Alone within a fellowship

In church, I found myself treated with suspicion when it was known I was separated or divorced. Many Christians have not examined the Scriptures to see what is really said about divorce, and therefore have only a vague idea about the rights and wrongs of it. Some saw any position of leadership as wrong, and others argued that if I married again my second husband would be an adulterer and so would I. Feeling condemned to a life of singleness and non-acceptance I was unprepared to justify myself to everyone, telling them the circumstances of my divorce. I found less tolerance, love and understanding and acceptance in the church than in the world.

My son lost his girlfriend because her mother protected her daughter against 'the sins of the fathers' being passed on through his sons. 'Like father like son!' I was told. I found myself being criticized for being friends with so many young people and viewed with suspicion if I dared laugh or joke with a young man. But the young people rallied around us. They were not afraid of being friends. They prayed for us and visited us and made life 'normal' for us.

How acutely aware I was that couples stopped inviting me to their homes, and women moved quickly to join us if I talked to their husbands. What did the poor women think I would do? People my own age were embarrassed to be with me because they did not know what to say.

Worst of all, no-one touched me – no hugs, no reassuring pats, no arms around the shoulder. It all seemed to confirm to me that I was unclean, untouchable, no good! I was so ashamed of being divorced, secretly feeling relieved my ex-husband was out of my life, but guilty because I felt that way. Typing out the verse from Jeremiah, I pinned it on my wardrobe where I could see it often.

Tender mercies

God was healing my children and releasing their talents and gifts. How I rejoiced when one by one they told me that their Heavenly Father had opened their eyes to what had happened in the family, showing them how I had been treated. Each asked forgiveness for their anger and accusations. We were able to learn the principles of forgiveness in practice. Once my family settled down, the pressure decreased and some of the hurt I had shelved began to surface. It is still my time to heal.

Discussing divorce with others who had gone through it made me realise patterns in my thinking that were destructive. Even my relationship with the Lord had changed. I did not feel sure I could trust him in the area of friendships and relationships. Repenting of my doubts and fears I started making friends again. Over time I was able to share to the point of vulnerability with one or two people I could trust. One morning, on a retreat, I put all my fears, hurts, anger, shelved dreams, faded vision and brokenness before the Lord, asking him to help me let go and to trust him with my life again. I asked him to bring all the shattered fragments of my inner life together and to make me whole. That, I believe, was a turning point for me. How much my loving Father has done in restoring me to wholeness.

I won't pretend that all is yet well with my

soul. Fears still surround relationships – can anyone really love me for who I am and not for what I can do for them? Facing the idea that I may have to live alone for the rest of my life is a continuing struggle. And I still fight against feelings of shame and condemnation for being divorced and a Christian. There are days when death seems an easy option. But ... I get up faster now than I used to! An elderly missionary once told me, 'The devil might kick you down, but don't lie there and let him wipe his feet on you!' As time passes I am learning to distinguish between God's truth and the whispered lies that are so easy to believe. In it all, I am learning to have hope again. God does have a future for me! He does have plans that are for my good, and he will bring peace back into my life!

My family is more grown up now and the eldest is happily married. Three of my children are studying at university, and independent. One still lives at home. They are happy, secure young people, well liked and respected by their peers and others who know them. I am deeply grateful to God for his healing in their lives.

5

KENNETH STEVEN

There is a battle being fought, and a very serious one. It is a battle for the hearts and minds of millions of ordinary people who are affected by the music they hear, the films they watch, and the books they read. As I am a writer I am primarily concerned with the last of these areas, but I know very well that what happens within publishing is linked to what is screened on television, what Hollywood produces, and what the music industry promotes. It is within this huge network that I find something frightening and insidious that is in danger of infecting the whole spectrum of the arts. Christians, and others in the arts world who stand against these current trends, are being shut out deliberately by those who have taken control of the movement. That is the battle in which I am engaged.

This account describes some of the wounds which have been inflicted on me, and the greatness of God who has sustained me throughout, even in the dark days when I could hardly feel his presence.

I was brought up in rural Perthshire by loving Christian parents. From my earliest days I can remember praying and being prayed for. The notion of Jesus being a friend became stronger and stronger until, while I was still quite small, it seemed the most natural thing in the world to commit my life to him. My involvement in Christian activities goes back to school days. Of particular importance to me were the house groups which my parents started and ran in the several communities in which we lived at different times. I enjoyed the wrestling with big questions; the way that faith was not static but always developing and progressing through struggles and learning.

A home full of typewriters!

Both my parents were writers. My father had always written for a living; by the time I was a teenager my mother had seen her first book published. I suppose, therefore, that the sound of the typewriter was one of the most common noises in the house when I was growing up, and by thirteen or so I was fighting to use one myself as I embarked on my first novel.

School days, particularly those from late primary to early secondary, were very unhappy indeed. Mental and physical bullying pushed me in on myself and meant that the world of my imagination became stronger and stronger. In time both my poetry and prose began to deal with suffering itself, reflecting both the hurt I felt and that which I perceived in others.

The Unborn, the first novel I ever completed, was a fantasy, yet about a very real and important issue. It told the story of children from this world who, aborted and destroyed by society, were reborn into a country where they were imprisoned by their own fear and bitterness, and with the full knowledge of what had brought them there. The novel tells of the Orpheus-like journey of two of the children to free their people from the chains of darkness. It is about the infinitely precious and God-given nature of life, and the terrible darkness that humanity has managed all too often to reduce that life to. In 1992, the year in which it was finally published – and that process was rendered much more difficult because of the book's Christian content – it was short-listed for the *Deo Gloria Award*.

My writing diverged from that of my parents. Whereas they were entirely concerned with non-fiction, with the production of articles and historical studies, I was far away in other worlds, slaying dragons and bringing back treasures. I think that, initially, this kind of writing was so important to me because of what was taking place outside our home. Having been badly bullied at both the senior secondary schools I attended in Perthshire, writing itself, and the escape it provided, became precious indeed. Here I could be in control of what took place, and I could act with courage through the characters I created, when in everyday life I felt small and insignificant and powerless.

However, I slowly moved away from fantasy fiction and began to become aware of my own landscapes. In the writing of Seamus Heaney and R S Thomas especially, I discovered how the ordinary and everyday experience of the country could be translated into the most magnificent poetry. In the novels of Neil Gunn I saw how the real suffering and struggle of past generations could be brought alive to a new generation. That was the direction in which my writing took me.

Suddenly that place rises
Sharp as a stag in my memory
The track winds round the hillside, out of sight
Like long ago childhood. I see boys going home
With silver shining trout, blue lochs
In their wide-spaced eyes and Gaelic songs
To strengthen the miles of summer midges.
Someone is gathering myrtle, a curlew longs
Over the deep acres of the sky and the lights
Like simple prayers shine out
In the homes that kneel by the loch.

Landscapes of the mind

My own first poems were drawing primarily on memories. I wanted to create landscapes with imagery, and to people those landscapes with portraits of those whose actions and words had become embedded in my mind. More and more of these poems were being chiselled from my years of association with the west and north, with a Gaelic world. Sometimes poems came to me in a single moment, were so vivid that my hands literally shook with emotion. Gradually I became aware that this gift was very much a double-edged sword, one whose intensity caused pain as well as delight. Often it wasn't a choice to write; words were there at four in the morning, 'being born' on to the page. And I was just the catalyst, the one honoured with holding the pen.

After, I suppose, several hundred poems had been published in outlets throughout Britain and abroad, my first collection, *Remembering Peter*, was brought out by the National Poetry Foundation. Now, a long time later, a further two collections have been published, and a volume of selected poems, *The Missing Days*. Perhaps what has been most exciting of all is to see poems appearing ever more regularly abroad; in the States, Canada and Australia particularly. God has given me much encouragement through these difficult years.

Capturing an inheritance

In those days when I was discovering my own identity as a writer, I began to realise that I too had an inheritance, that my experience of Highland culture, of rural Scotland, was of infinite worth; that what I had seen and heard in my childhood had to be captured before it was lost from memory. I wanted to write about Gaelic culture and the people of the north because I wanted to express my gratitude to God for all that was good in this Highland existence, for the reverence there was for the land and its life. I wanted to capture with words some of the finest people I had known in childhood, people who had been close to God and who had reverence and love for creation, whose eyes could fill with light at the sound of a skein of geese passing overhead, and with reluctant admiration even when a family of young rabbits were stealing their last carrots in the early morning.

Faith in the face of adversity, the struggle between humanity and God and between people themselves, those were the things I longed to write about, to find expression for the important, the elemental things that made up the human condition: love, conflict, anger, forgiveness and laughter itself. I wanted to write about universals, so as to understand and to be able to piece together something of the whole experience of being alive in this world.

Culture shock

But at university I discovered abruptly that this kind of writing was neither wanted nor considered 'politically correct'. The contemporary literature I studied portrayed working class experience at its rawest and often most savage. James Kelman was the hero of our times; our lecturers praised his writing to the skies and most students did not deviate from that party line. When I took my best poems to the Professor of English Literature, he systematically tore them to shreds. How very alone I felt in what I was writing. I really had no allies at all, and I found it hard to justify my subject matter and style to the 'urbo-centric' young writers around me. At least for some of Kelman's writings there seemed to be a moral framework and a purpose, but what began to be clear to me was that for the new generation of young writers following in his wake there was no purpose whatsoever behind the despair.

I could well understand that it was valid to give a voice to the thousands of dispossessed and disillusioned in the inner city schemes, and to illustrate how they had been trapped by an ever-worsening spiral of gang culture and violent, drug-related crime. But these writers were totally nihilistic; they portrayed violence and often sadistic cruelty with a voyeur's indulgence. To them there were no answers to the violence and the drugs; they were the answers themselves.

Opposite extremes

My new novel *Dan* was, therefore, almost a direct and deliberate statement of opposition to this writing. It was the story of the last day in the life of a hill farmer as he walked the circumference

81

of his land. Each part of that land awakens memories; in chronological order we learn of the events that have made up his life, and in completing the circle of that life we meet also its death. *Dan* is a lament for all that was and is precious and reverent in the Highland way of life; Dan himself becomes a symbol of the loss of that world. It warns of the wrong directions we have taken and are taking; it points backwards, and upwards. It seems to me that in Scotland particularly we are seeing increasingly a monoculture of the *Trainspotting* genre of writing. And it is not solely writing, as I have said before. *Trainspotting* was famous as a book, then as a film, then later still for its music. But I am frightened. I am frightened that a growing literary mafia is taking hold to promote the works of those artists, and perhaps more importantly, to keep out the work of those who are opposed to this culture. More and more publishers are yielding to the temptation to follow this trend; to bring out material that is marketable primarily for its 'shockability'. This new writing is already on the school curriculum.

As a young and struggling writer, where did I find myself? One group of individuals held sway over a generation's creativity. The so-called realism of cult novels, films and even television series is very subjective. Not everyone in the inner city uses violence to escape from difficulty or from situations they find hard to deal with; not everyone turns to drugs and crime because they have the misfortune to endure the hardships of a poor background. And to suggest that they do seems to me to be patronising to say the least! Against that backdrop I wrote on, often using *Dan* as a model for my new writing, only to find that goodness, love, trust, forgiveness, compassion and faith were perceived as romantic notions by the creators of this 'real' world. Was it, I wondered, fear of such concepts that made the literary minded marginalise and mock them? They seemed to live in a world where valuable things were trivialised, and trivial and petty things were awarded a status they did not merit.

Overcome by darkness

The books of C S Lewis had underpinned my childhood reading. As a young man I appreciated more deeply Lewis' perceptiveness in his novel, *The Last Battle*, in which people eventually believe in the darkness around them; ceasing to see anything but the darkness. I appreciated it – and shuddered at the thought.

In that story, the dwarves have been inside a cramped stable whose walls are suddenly and miraculously removed. The dwarves are now essentially on lush grass, with blue sky and tall trees around them. Yet they continue to sit there cramped and huddled together, convinced they are still in the dark filth of the stable. They are then given a veritable feast to satisfy them – pies and sweet dishes and wine – but they cannot taste any more. One says he was trying to eat hay, another an old turnip, and a third a cabbage leaf. This is nothing less than a portrayal of hell, a self-created hell, which no-one can be persuaded to leave against his will.

I was reminded of Lewis' picture when I watched a video concerning the influence of screen violence on youngsters in Scandinavia. One girl who was interviewed lived in the far north of Sweden in an under populated region of forest and lake. Because of her fear of being attacked while on her own at any time, she had taken to carrying a broken bottle with her wherever she went. And if you tell people this is the way it is everywhere, and if eventually they believe you, the danger is exactly this, that they will begin to behave as if it is true. This is the world in which I as a Christian writer live, and for which I, as a Christian writer, write.

Maintaining integrity

For a time I kept my head beneath the parapet; I thought it was better to slog on doggedly, hoping the literary mafia might eventually recognise my limited success and admit me to their ranks. But then I realised that I myself and others were being shut out deliberately, from publication, grants, air-time – a voice, in fact, of any kind. I was once commissioned to review a book for one of the major literary magazines in Scotland, a novel by one of the notorious younger writers, some of it so downright horrific it was hard to read. I said as much in my review, though my criticism was rational and quite controlled. The editor, with great embarrassment, wrote to me saying he would not be publishing my piece and would be offering the reviewing task to someone else. He didn't like that fact that I had dared to criticise this young novelist whose work everyone else had praised to the skies.

I know that I am not the only writer or artist in the country today who feels their work is well-nigh censored. But I realise now I do not want to be accepted by them, that it is my duty to fight against them. In 1996 I wrote a short piece on the subject for a national newspaper, imagining it would not find favour. To my great surprise the editor answered by return, inviting me to provide an essay for the weekend paper. For the first time I had an opportunity to describe the situation precisely as I saw it. I no longer minded who might be opening up a new file on me; I felt I had joined a battle, that I had crossed a very small Rubicon and would not be going back.

To my delight, I received a whole series of letters in support of what I had written. Others were realising that the tide had to turn, that this state of affairs could not be allowed to continue indefinitely. I even received a letter from one of the young novelists whose work I had been indirectly taking to task in the article. He admitted that he had never before seen things in that light and that I had been courageous in writing as I had.

Writing for the real world

There are so many issues that are crying out to be taken up by our writers and artists today, especially our Christian writers and artists. We live in a western society bombarded by news of the chaos and suffering of our neighbours. We are not close to finding lasting solutions to world hunger, to the destruction of our natural resources and this jewel of an earth, with its rain forests and myriad species that have been shaped by an awesome and wondrous Creator.

> Three hours from Brazilia
> Through the black hum of the night
> He looked down from the plane and saw circles
> Blazing edges of orange, here and there
> Through the nowhere of the dark, eerie
> All the way to the northern coast
> Till the plane tilted into morning and drifted down
> Beside the opal rim of the sea.
>
> It was only later he remembered the fires
> Realised at last he had seen
> The rainforest burning.

That is why it is so incongruous that much of today's creativity is concerned with sadistic violence and sordid fantasy. Stories and even poetry are designed to shock. We have the world at our fingertips and seem unmoved in the midst of the suffering. Society is looking inward at its own darkness; consumers crave to discover new types of entertainment and more pleasures with which to push away the awareness of inner emptiness and fear of death.

So Christian witness, the power of salt and light, is ever more vital. So it must be for me and others like me in the world of the arts; not abandoning creativity, but rather using it to impart a vision of hope and transformation. It was God who made the imagination, and though it can and has been used for great wrong, it can illuminate and inspire and awaken. That is where I am as a Christian writer. Along with my brothers and sisters in the world of the arts we must be prophets, speaking of the pain and wrongness of secular society and of what ultimately matters to our audience.

But it is a fight, and an exhausting one, standing up against the trend when large numbers have clearly conformed in order to receive the recognition and funding they so urgently require. It is my hope that an alliance of like-minded individuals can be gathered which others will join, encouraged by the knowledge they are not alone.

In the arts world as anywhere else, it is so often the crowd mentality which prevails. Artists like to be part of movements; they want confirmation of their opinions and their statements, especially when they are daring to go against the establishment of their day.

We who take a stand against the very real evil being propagated in this arts world today have the strongest ally of all on our side, Christ himself. There can be no guarantee either of victory in our day or of fame; it is the fight itself, the stand which matters.

'Finally, brothers, whatever is true, whatever is noble, whatever is right, whatever is pure, whatever is lovely, whatever is admirable – if anything is excellent or praiseworthy – think about such things' (Philippians 4:8).

6

LENA COWIE

David Robert Cowie was born at 11.30 am on 15th October 1984 in Inverness. That day changed our lives in ways we could not have imagined. For me David was different from before he was born. I had a difficult pregnancy but a busy one as we had three teenagers and two little ones, and I had a manse to run. My husband, Alex, was minister of Creich, Kincardine and Croick Free Churches in the north of Scotland. David came twelve weeks early and was delivered by caesarean section. I remember the night vividly: the forty mile ambulance journey to Inverness with Elspeth and Cathy, our village nurses, seemed endless. I prayed that the Lord would look after my baby. For I feared for him.

David was four days old before I saw him and I was shocked when I did. His face was covered in cotton pads, and a ventilator, taped to his cheeks and ears, filled his mouth. He had a feeding tube in his nose and tubes into his wrists and legs. His tiny arms were pulled through the opening of the incubator. He was restless, trying to cry, but unable to. I stroked his arms and legs. They were so soft. Comforted, he lay still. I stayed as long as my little strength lasted.

In my weariness I thought on Bible verses I knew. One kept coming to mind, 'He that believeth shall not make haste' (Isaiah 28:16, AV). It upset me. When a Christian nurse brought me a missionary magazine a rush of anger filled me as I read, 'He that believeth shall not make haste.' Although I knew in my heart it was God's speaking, I confess with shame that I threw down the magazine exclaiming, 'That's not what I want.'

Although Alex came most days, sometimes I did not even remember his visits. Nor did I see the children who were at home being well looked after by Alex's mother. It was so strange. I had a baby, but did not really have him. Other people cared for him as I looked on. David seemed to be improving. He used the ventilator less till he was taken off it and breathed unaided. But the following day his lungs collapsed and my poor baby was ventilated again.

Still ... but still alive

When I went to see him the following morning doctors and nurses surrounded David's incubator. Our baby lay completely still and deathly pale. My mind cried out that the Lord had taken him away, and my knees turned to jelly. But David was alive. One of his lungs had collapsed. I could not understand why the Lord felt so far from helping me. I wept. I prayed, asking God to help me submit to his perfect plan for David. It was then God spoke though his word, 'This sickness is not unto death, but for the glory of God' (John 11:4, AV). I knew then that David would be spared to us for God's glory. And I cried again, but different tears. David's lungs collapsed for a third time before he was eventually able to breathe unaided.

I had not always looked to God for help. Although Alex and I were brought up to attend church we fell away in our teens. It was when our older children were small, and even then only when nagged by my parents, that I asked Mrs Stone, the minister's wife, about baptism. I didn't have the courage to ask the minister! She arranged for her husband to visit, and it was as a result of that visit I started going to church. I found I could not get enough of the Word of the Lord from which Rev Kenneth Stone preached. My interest did not please Alex, who was then a fisherman. But God worked in his heart too. Unknown to me he was reading a Bible Mrs Stone had given me. It was a difficult time for us both, but by the end of it we had found full and free forgiveness and new life in Jesus Christ. And it was on our relationship with him that we now had to rely in our time of need.

Two weeks after David's birth I went home,

leaving him in hospital. Esther was thirteen months old, and I shall never forget her wee face, she could not believe her eyes. Eleanor, aged four, sat on my knee, her eyes asking 'Is it really you?' Carl, Steven and Evelyn were so good and helpful. Unfortunately Alex had to go into hospital the very first week I was home. How hard that was, although I knew people were praying for us in all the neighbouring villages and I felt greatly upheld. But a nightmare was about to begin.

The phone rang one evening. I was needed urgently at Raigmore. David had developed *Hydrocephalus* and they had to find a blood match before sending him to the Special Baby Unit in Aberdeen. When I arrived at the hospital the bump on David's head was clearly visible. I held my helpless little baby for the first time, my heart breaking and tears coursing down my cheeks. The doctor handed me a box of tissues. 'You'll go through a lot of them,' he said, 'before this is over.' He was right. Another doctor went to the Royal Infirmary, where Alex was still a patient, to explain to him that the neurosurgeon would put a shunt, or valve, into David's head to clear the build-up of fluid. God gave us someone to help us in our great need. Ken Larter, who was then Free Church minister of Brora but who had previously been a nurse, was a great support through that crisis and throughout the long months that followed.

From Inverness to Aberdeen and back

David suffered several fits on the way to Aberdeen. By the time I saw him he was on anticonvulsant treatment and asleep almost constantly. I had to meet that situation alone as Alex was still too unwell to travel to Aberdeen. Surgery was carried out and was thought to have been successful, but the fluid was too thick to flow freely through the shunt and David was taken back to theatre. He was so pale and helpless. I could only look on and do nothing for him, nothing, that is, but love him and leave him in the Lord's care. The shunt still did not work and his head size increased alarmingly. He was pained and distressed. It was agony watching him.

I felt lost, bewildered and devastated. But I kept hanging on, if at times weakly, to the promise I had received from the Lord at the beginning, 'This sickness is not unto death, but for the glory of God.' I went to stay with Alex MacDonald, then Free Church minister in Aberdeen, and his wife, Evelyn, for the weekend. How much their kindly support meant to me. The situation became so bad and so distressing that I remember asking Alex, 'Is David still my child while he's in there?'

Despite everything that was being done David was not better but worse. In response to my saying, 'If you can do no more for David and he is going to die I want to take him home,' I was told, 'Oh no, Mrs Cowie, we don't think he is going to die, but at best you are going to have a healthy cabbage.'

'So be it,' I said, and walked away. I had reached rock bottom.

By the following Sunday Alex was fit to travel and we both went to Aberdeen to see our poor little son. When we had to return home the prognosis was far from encouraging. We agreed to ask the Lord specifically to make the shunt work that very day, to show his power where human effort and expertise had failed. Alex prayed over David then we left, committing him into God's care. That evening when I phoned the baby unit, I was told, 'The shunt appears to be working.' We fell to our knees in thanksgiving.

David was sent back to Inverness by ambulance a few days later and, because I could not travel the 80 miles round trip to feed him, on 21st December, aged nearly 10 weeks, David came home. Before long I was exhausted. David was still on anticonvulsant treatment and slept most of the day, but he was awake for hours during the night. I was reading at this time about King David, and my David would lie in my arms looking at me as if to say, 'What are you doing?' So I started to read aloud and he lay listening to my voice with obvious interest. The Lord encouraged me greatly in this. David would learn.

A few months later, in the summer of 1985, David was back in Raigmore Hospital following a build-up of fluid in his neck where the catheter entered the shunt. He was operated on and the shunt repaired. By this time he was off anti-convulsant treatment and thankfully has never needed it since. The name of our son's condition, *Cerebral Palsy*, started coming to the fore. Prior to that nobody had mentioned it. I read every book I could find on the subject. David's development was disappointing. He was unable to sit, crawl or roll over. Our three oldest children struggled with the question, 'Why is God doing this?' Such a situation as we were in raises problems and questions far beyond the practicalities of living with it.

David's consultant at Raigmore was a great help and encouragement. He authorised all the equipment David needed at home: seats, standing frames, even a tricycle which David could cycle under supervision, as he had to be strapped into it. How he loved his bike. Physiotherapy, however unwelcome from his point of view, did our son a great deal of good. And our visits to the Physiotherapy Department of the Child Development Unit gave me an insight into the struggles that face parents of a disabled child, from some people's hard and bitter attitudes to feelings of disappointment and concern.

Because, by the age of two years and nine months David could not sit or crawl, though he could feed himself, Esther and I went with him to the Raeden Centre for Child Development in Aberdeen for David to have intensive therapy and assessment in all aspects of child development. On the first evening we all went for a walk in the hospital grounds, and the first person we met was the doctor who had warned me our son would be just a healthy cabbage. 'Oh Mrs Cowie, how are you?' 'I'm well, thank you.' 'And David?' David said, 'I'm fine, Doctor. I'm down to visit the Raeden Centre with Mam and Esther. They're going to assess me to tell Mam how I will be.' The doctor said nothing. He looked at David, stroked his hair, then turned to me and said, 'It would appear I was wrong.' And he walked away.

The time spent at the Raeden Centre was both informative and helpful to me in learning about David's future needs and their management. I met many parents who were in the same position as us and who were in great anguish regarding their children. Some found it hard to see beyond the disability. They had still to learn to see their child first and the struggles that resulted from their child's disabilities after that.

Calming David's fears ... and mine
By the time David was eight years old he had undergone eight operations, riding to most of them on a Thomas the Tank Engine theatre trolley. I always stayed with him and he handled each one reasonably well. But, as he grew older and more

aware of what was happening, he became frightened. Then he would say to me, 'Mam, read to me and pray with me.' David loved singing psalms, especially psalm nine, which he knew by heart. At such times I found it very hard not to allow my apprehensions to overcome me. If they had done I would have been no help or encouragement to my child. But perhaps there were times when my voice shook as I sang his favourite psalm to him:

Lord, thee I'll praise with all my heart,
thy wonders all proclaim.
In thee, most High, I'll greatly joy,
and sing unto thy name.

God also will a refuge be
for those that are oppress'd;
A refuge will he be in times
of trouble to distress'd.

And they that know thy name, in thee
their confidence will place;
For thou hast not forsaken them
that truly seek thy face.

O sing ye praises to the Lord
that dwells in Sion hill;
And all the nations among
his deeds record ye still.

(Psalm 9: 1-2, 9-11)
Scottish Metrical Version of the Psalms)

It is emotionally draining when your child is hanging on to you and screaming, 'Mam, help me,' before the effects of an anaesthetic start to work. No doubt, like many other mothers and fathers, I found the corridors long and lonely. But I always felt upheld and strengthened by God's Word. It reminded me that my times, and David's times, are in the hands of the God who made us and who cares for us even more than we care for each other.

When David was three and a half years old, in answer to our prayers, the Lord provided Phyllis Ross as my home help. We did not know it then, but she was to be a great help to David. Because he was unable to get around in the normal way he devised his own method of moving from room to room. He lay on his back and manoeuvred himself with his head and legs. He delighted to watch Phyllis dust and hoover the manse. David was 'hooked on hoovering'. Steven bought him a toy upright hoover which we went round with daily thus making his contribution to keeping things clean. It is easy to imagine how a strong friendship soon developed between Phyllis and David. 'My boy,' she would say. I shared with her all that I had learned and was learning about different ways of helping David to improve his motor skills.

And so to school
God's care did not end with the provision of Phyllis. When David went to nursery the teacher

'happened' to have had experience with physically impaired children, and a great love for them. Mrs Bremner worked very hard with David, and Mrs Gillanders, her helper, did likewise. As they were also close friends of the infant teacher his time at nursery provided a good springboard for entering primary one at Bonar Bridge Primary School. It was necessary for David to have a full time attendant in main stream schooling. Phyllis, although she had no educational qualifications, was ideally suited to the position and we strongly encouraged her to apply. She did, and the local education authority had the good sense to appoint her. This proved to be a highly successful arrangement because of her previous knowledge and experience of David, coupled with her willingness to learn from the therapists and infant teacher. Speaking of therapists, Anne was a great support, and both she and Jeanette helped David a great deal. Then Marion came to work in the north. She was Bobath trained and was very pleased with David's progress, though he did not always appreciate her efforts on his behalf! This particular kind of physiotherapy can be of great benefit to children who suffer from *Cerebral Palsy*.

David enjoyed school. Mrs Chisholm, 'his teacher' as he called her, was very fond of him and they still keep in touch. She worked exceptionally hard to help him. David loved his teacher and, despite his learning difficulties, gained a lot from his time with her. Mrs Chisholm was also our nearest neighbour as her husband had the croft near the manse. David loved going there. He helped feed the cows and did the rounds with Sandy, watching him carry out his chores. Trips on the tractor were a great treat at harvest time and when the peats came home in summer.

Despite David's physical and educational difficulties he communicates well, and is a very friendly and outgoing boy with a great sense of humour and a real concern for other people. He also has an extraordinary gift – he never, ever forgets names and faces. This can be very useful when I do! The David we know and love is gregarious, giggly, and great fun to have around. But for those interested in a more technical classification of his condition, he is regarded as a *moderately severe asymmetrical spastic quad-riplegic*, with the right side more involved.

Some people think that disabled children need to be treated differently from 'normal' children. Alex and I have never adopted that approach. David has been brought up just the same as our other children: to accept the Bible's teaching, that God knows best in behaviour, relationships, discipline, respect etc. From his earliest days David has taken part in the joys and sorrows of life. And he goes wherever we go. As a result he has been to places in his wheelchair where many able-bodied children have never been. David has watched seabirds nesting on, and flying off, the cliffs in Westray, Orkney. He has collected eggs from the hen house and fed pet lambs. With us he has visited Mull, Iona, Skye, Lewis and Harris, to name but a few places of which we have happy memories.

One area of human experience David finds upsetting is change. He has known much of it in the family, with his brothers and one of his sisters moving away for further education then to set up their homes, the loss of dear folk in the congregation, and the deep sadness of losing both his grandfathers within two weeks of each other. Then there was the upset of leaving his beloved home in Migdale in 1995, to come with his three sisters, Eleanor, Esther and Mirian, who are still at home, to live in Glasgow when Alex moved to Christian service there. David has settled into his new life and surroundings very well. But he misses the Highlands and loves going back on holiday.

Looking back and looking forward

David has brought a great deal of joy, hard work and understanding of handicap to us all. He has changed our lives. How much the Lord has taught us all through him: to be more loving and under-standing, more thankful and prayerful, and to see the funny side of life. I am so thankful to God who in his mercy spared David to us. And when I hear him pray for others much more able than himself I have to say, 'It is better to take refuge in the Lord than to trust in man' (Psalm 118:8).

To my dear husband and my loving children who have worked so hard and helped so much, I shall always be grateful. There are also so many good friends who prayed for us at the throne of grace and still do, to whom I feel a deep sense of gratitude. Finally, and most importantly, I ask myself: 'How can I repay the Lord for all his goodness to me?', and respond with the psalm writer, 'I will lift up the cup of salvation and call on the name of the LORD' (Psalm 116:12-13).

7

RACHEL AND KATE

Rachel introduces herself and her sister
Kate and I are sisters, close in age, and close to each other. We grew up in a 'manse family'. Both parents were Christians and perhaps, for two or three years after my birth, all appeared well within their marriage. Then, suddenly, our father left. Out of the blue, or so it seemed, he no longer loved our mother, could not live with us any more, and was in love with a member of the congregation. He left. For twelve years, from the ages of three and five, we saw him at weekends.

Our childhood years, by Kate
The first few years of my parents' marriage were, I believe, fairly difficult for both of them. They had come from very different backgrounds, had differing expectations of what it meant to live as Christians, and very different personalities. I also believe that it was the first time that my father had ever had to face any real problem in life, and that, confronted with a difficult marriage, his response was to run away.

As a result of the family splitting up, my

mother, sister and I moved from the manse to a semi-detached house. My mother had to work full-time, although her preference would have been to enjoy being at home with 'her girls'. Despite being without our father the years following the break-up were happy ones for the two of us, although I am sure this must have been a desolate time for our mother. Many years later, when we were both adults, she told us about her complete reliance on the presence and strength of God through all the years of being a single parent, but especially in the early years of the break-up.

Our childhood years were, I think, sheltered. We attended a very 'middle class' primary school and, although the other pupils knew our father was not around, it was never talked about, nor were we ever made to feel that we were odd or different in any way. I do recall, however, one teacher and a parent of one of my best friends asking questions after we had visited Dad at weekends. These made me feel very uneasy, although I didn't understand why. While there is a place for showing interest in a child's life, children will normally tell you what they want you to know, and I discovered at that early age how pressured such questioning can make a child feel.

On one occasion, while on holiday, we were playing on swings with two sisters. The girls asked repeated questions about where our dad was, eventually developing a chant of, 'Where's your dad?'

then, 'Don't you have a dad?' This may appear to be a tiny incident but I can still feel the hurt and discomfort of these moments. No doubt the girls involved forgot it.

These years must have been very difficult ones for our mother: at the age of thirty three she was coping with two young children, a new house, church and town, financial constraint, loneliness, and various advances from non-Christian men who must have considered her fair game for a relationship, and Christian friends who found it difficult to support a divorcee. Mum did, in fact, make some very supportive and faithful friends over these years, but many of those friends who had been closest when our parents were married, withdrew.

Rachel now understands
To us, as children, the prospect of our mum remarrying filled us with terror and despair. We reacted quite differently to her friends. One of us, with sweetness and grace, accepted kindly any male friends she had. The other, sulking and refusing to be nice or friendly in any way, made life as difficult as possible for all. Of course, fear of losing the most important person in our lives to some stranger was the reason. We needed to be treated differently. For me, the best approach was to ignore my sulks and rudeness and to plug on, with reassurance, but also total honesty, and with

105

no hidden agendas or plans. Even children know when something is afoot. Openness and unconditional love, often expressed, are the keys.

Mourning a loss, says Kate

There was a sort of mourning process, a coming to terms with the loss of my father and, as I saw it, the loss of half of my family. Driving in the car with mum, she told me that she and dad were divorced. I felt as if the world slowed down, and I became an observer, looking down on a play in which I was taking part. I woke up that night crying, mourning the loss. We are rightly patient with children who have suffered bereavement; perhaps we could bear other losses in mind which may not seem so final to us, but are to the children or young people concerned.

The secondary school we attended was very different from our primary experience. The catchment area included some areas of deprivation and suddenly, my sister and I were among many young people who came from non-nuclear families. Yet we still felt 'different' and vulnerable.

Both my sister and I became Christians in our early teens and, from that point onwards, our lifestyles differed greatly from those of our friends. We chose not to drink alcohol or go out to nightclubs, spending most of our spare time with school friends. We were very fortunate to be part of a good group of young people from

Christian families, and a church which organised a youth club and youth fellowship for us. This gave us somewhere interesting to go on a Saturday night. It has been said that young people like to run in a pack, and that if they are not given a pack to run in, they will find one! We both benefited from the encouragement we received in our Christian peer group as we faced the increasingly secular environment in which we lived.

Rachel reflects on practicalities

I think society is now more aware of 'broken homes' and 'single parent families'. Perhaps situations such as I found myself in when registering for secondary school no longer arise. I remember clearly sitting, almost in tears, trying to fill in a form which asked for 'father's name and occupation'. I knew that I wanted to put my mum's name down, that my father was not the one to contact in an emergency – but I was too young and scared to know what to do. 'If anyone has problems, come to my desk,' said the unknown teacher, a young man, at the front of the class. I went forward. All eyes in the new class followed me. One other girl also went up. 'My dad died,' she said. 'That's fine, just put your mum's name down.' I wished my situation was so clear cut and 'acceptable'. 'My dad doesn't live with us,' I muttered. I don't know what the poor man thought, but he gave me the same advice. A simple rephrasing of the form to 'parent' rather than 'father' would have been enough. Perhaps this is the case in these sad days of more family break-ups. I certainly hope it is now easier for those affected by such circumstances. It is a lesson we can all take to our workplaces, homes and pulpits – thinking ourselves into the position of an uncertain child, and working to ease any pain or stigma.

Insecure? Yes, agrees Kate

My sister's example of feeling different because of the wording on a form brings a vivid memory to my mind. A well-meaning Guidance teacher once asked me in an interview what my father did. She then enquired why I had put my mother's name down as parent or guardian on a form. I answered, blushing, and hoped desperately that she would leave it at that. Thankfully, she did. Did I feel insecure about our situation? I think I must have done. I certainly felt much more comfortable within the church family than outside of it.

Coping with divorce – Rachel's thoughts

Visiting our father became more difficult when we went into senior school, as increasingly Saturdays were in demand for hockey, tennis and Saturday jobs. But it was on one such visit that the bombshell was dropped. Our father announced that he was going to marry the woman he had been involved with since leaving us. We were fifteen and seventeen years old. Feeling that it was cowardly to tell us this news when we were away from home, and before telling our mother, we cut short that visit. He phoned our mother before we arrived back and she was, understandably, very upset. When he had left us at our home we sat and cried and discussed the past, what to do now and in the future, and decided that visiting would no longer be possible. Whether this was the right decision we don't know to this day. We differ as to how to approach our relationship with our father.

Then came the end of school. Kate went to university not far from home, and two years later I became a student, just a bit further distant. The bonds between 'the three girls' could not have been closer. The consequences of our father's actions were many – the closeness we shared in growing up, and the struggles both within the church family and with other authorities, school and friends, made us quite a team. My sister and I could turn our hands to anything around the home: gardening, repairs, changing plugs and carrying suitcases. This led to a strong belief in equality of ability and opportunity for women. No task was male or female for us – we were all female and life went on. This has led to us having strong views about the church's attitude in some areas with regard to what are perceived to be male and female roles.

Often in the church much is made of the traditional family – father, mother and 2.4 children. Children's addresses, for example, 'It's Father's Day today, and what did you all give Daddy this morning?' – without thought of those who have no father, and for whom this cuts like a knife. I believe the idea is that, if we keep to ideal scenarios and lay on or repeat traditional family patterns, it confirms that we value the family as a unit and as God's best way. Of course this is true, but Jesus also came for the orphan, the widow and the poor. Sensitivity is so important in the church setting, in 'family services' and in all we say from our positions of leadership or friendship. I think society in general is more aware and sensitive; how sad it would be if the church were not.

There are more questions than answers in relation to divorce. What, for example, do you say when, aged eighteen and a new student, a Christian minister and his wife, whom you have never met before, approach you and say, 'You don't know us, but we knew your parents at university. We lost touch – it was all so difficult, you know, what with the divorce.' What I said amounted to the fact that it had been more difficult for those in the situation, and that our mum could have done with more support. I said it kindly, and read in their faces a mixture of guilt and revelation.

It seems to me that people are generally ignorant of the needs and feelings of Christian families who feel that divorce is not God's way, but who find it has happened to them, and that life is a struggle physically, financially, and against stigma and ignorance within both the church and society generally. Single parents need support, friendship and inclusion. They don't need couples who won't get involved for fear of their narrow views being challenged, or because it's nice for couples to socialise together, and a single divorcee is a threat or difficult to place socially.

Kate benefits from hindsight

We both went to university at the age of eighteen. I lived in halls of residence for the first two years and returned home to live in third year, largely because our mother was left on her own and I felt it was right for me to be with her. It was a difficult time, and I resented having to give up part of my life for someone else. At the age of twenty, the repercussions of the broken marriage were continuing. Perhaps if my father had been able to see, or had considered, the far-reaching consequences of his decision to leave his family, he would have thought again.

My experience has taught me the importance of couples who are intending to marry talking to each other, and talking to someone wise and experienced with whom they can be honest. I understand that both my parents had major doubts about their relationship before they were married, and that neither of them felt they could express their feelings to the other. Perhaps if they had been able to speak openly about these matters with each other or a trusted friend, the outcome of their relationship would have been different.

Rachel fills in the facts

Both of us finished university and went on to further training colleges, and jobs. When we were in our early twenties, our mum remarried, to a Christian widower whom she met at church. We were more or less away from the nest by that stage and were very pleased for them both, although new relationships require time, and more time to develop.

Brokenhearted ... Kate tells their moving story

When I was twenty nine, our mother died. It was a relatively short illness, I suppose, of two years, which was easier for all of us in some ways though harder in others. It is a grinding sorrow to see a person you love gradually becoming weaker and more taken over by illness. Our mother had often spoken of her sense of being supported by God over the years, and of her belief that she had survived only because she had been upheld by his strength. Her total trust in the Lord was evident in the way she faced up to each stage of her ill-

112

ness, and finally in her complete confidence that she was about to go home to be with him for ever.

I felt very much alone during the latter stages of Mum's illness. I now know that God was always beside me, but that I held him away or shut him out. Perhaps I was angry with him for allowing this awful thing to happen, and confused that he did not stop the progress of the disease. All my fears blocked out the feeling of his presence. But in times like these, while God may appear to be absent or silent, he is right beside us. In fact, we need to believe that God is present no matter what we feel or don't feel at the time.

After our mother died, I continued to feel empty and removed from God. I was very angry with him. After all, we only had one parent. Why did other people still have two, and the only one we had was gone? Since then, I've learned that there is no answer to that question. But I do believe that there is a reason known to God why our mother had to die at that time, and I can even see some good things which have happened since. My view now is that God loves us much, much more than anyone else, and that our job is to trust him no matter what happens. It is easy to say this, but I think that, for me, it is the only way to understand what happened. I consider Job, and the fact that no-one could work out the reason for the terrible events which overtook him (though many tried!), yet it was God's plan, and his reasoning is perfect.

**'You never get over the death of your mother.'
Rachel agrees**

Our mother's death from breast cancer is another chapter entirely; the saddest most soul-wrenching time of loss. Much could be said – she was a fine Christian lady who gave her life to bring us up in the faith, and besides that, was our best and closest friend. Now, nearly five years later, the dreadful emptiness and apathy of the first two years has subsided; but the tears still come, and the loss is still felt keenly. At the time someone said, 'You never get over the loss of your mother.' It is a simple thought, but so sadly true. Perhaps for those without a mother, brought up by a father, the wording could be altered. We missed her so much at Kate's wedding. But for Mother, to be with God is better by far.

Kate's story

I married at the age of thirty three. For some years I perceived a pressure to marry, and I am sure that some Christians marry because of a fear of not meeting another suitable partner. I was 'encouraged' to settle for someone for many years. The arguments given included that the person was 'reasonable' and that he 'wasn't a bad package!' It is very difficult indeed to wait until you are sure that you have met the person you believe is the right one for you. But I am sure I was right to do so.

114

My husband and I now live in an old sandstone flat. He is a lovely, gentle Christian man, and I feel that God has given me my 'heart's desire'. Both of us come from broken homes, both our fathers having left their families. And my husband, too, lost his mother two years ago. We are aware that each of us carries emotional and psychological baggage into our marriage. But we also bring an awareness that Christian marriages do split up and that there is an enormous amount of hard work to be done to make a relationship a success. I hope that knowing the far reaching consequences of one partner leaving a marriage will make us both work harder and persevere toward making ours a success.

'Wise judgement,' cautions Rachel

As Christ forgave us, so we must come to a position of peace with ourselves, with God over the issue, and with our father. Whether it is mandatory to seek an ongoing relationship with a parent who severed the rights and responsibilities of parenthood by abandonment, is, I think, unclear, and a matter for wise judgment. It may take years to forgive. We cannot forget. But we must find peace, forgiveness, and learn from our experiences. In so doing we may help others to understand, and be Christ's hands here on earth.

Kate's concluding thoughts

I meet up with my father fairly regularly. Our relationship is, I think, a good one in that we exchange news and are open with each other, both about the past and about what is happening now in our lives. I believe I have forgiven him for leaving. But the feelings of hurt and anger may never completely disappear. We are friends who care for each other. I think that, realistically, is the best that can be hoped for.

It has been a helpful exercise for me to write this account. I feel that I have relived some experiences in the process, and it has enabled me to think through issues again. My sister and I hope and pray that what we have shared may be of help to someone who is going through a similar experience now, or who has done so in the past, or who does not quite know how best to relate to a friend who is in this position.

8

W VERNON HIGHAM

I shall begin my story by giving a brief outline of my background. At present I am the minister of Heath Evangelical Church at Cardiff where I have been for the last thirty-five years. My place of birth was Caernarfon in north west Wales and my early childhood was spent there. The times were hard for many people during the depression of the 1930s, but in some ways our family's lot seemed better than most because we had a grocer's shop in the town and a market garden with a large poultry farm outside the town. However, in those days nothing prospered and as a result, like so many of our fellow countrymen, we left Wales to find a livelihood elsewhere. My father decided that as a family we should return to his former home town in the north of England. It was a dramatic change from a Welsh market town to a large industrial town in Lancashire. For the next few years Bolton was our home and we became part of the large Welsh community in the Manchester area, with its network of Welsh chapels. It was a change of language, a change of surroundings and a change of schools.

Then the war came, with all its limitations and anxieties, and towards the end of it I reached the 'call-up' age. We were allowed to give our preference for the three branches of the services and the order that I chose was the army, the navy, the air-force. To my surprise I found myself, together with all the other young men of my group, in the coal mines! It was a very interesting experience and I am grateful for it. Afterwards I continued my education and was trained as a school teacher in Trinity College, Carmarthen. During the time I spent there, and looking back later, I can say that they were very happy years. Having enjoyed the course, I loved teaching and made so many friends. I then taught Welsh in Cardiff, and after a while returned home to Lancashire and taught there for a few years. During this time I had a mild degree of asthma but it did not limit my activities in any way.

Searching and finding

It is my belief that God had been working in my life for some considerable time. I had always attended chapel regularly, both services and Sunday School, and in addition the prayer meeting and other meetings we held during the week. Loving the chapel as I did I would never think of doing anything else on the Lord's day. Yet for all that, there was something missing – I used to describe it as a piano without the middle C, or the lost chord in my life. I desperately wanted to know God and to be at peace with him. My quest started in earnest while I was in Cardiff. During a time of illness I became particularly anxious and made God a promise to serve him when I recovered. It was this that prompted me to return home to my parents and tell them quietly of my intentions. My spiritual motives were unclear. I believe that it was partly to please God and partly in the hope that I would find what I was looking for.

Although in my childhood I had been surrounded by the 1904 Revival people, I knew nothing of salvation in a real way or of assurance of salvation. To leave teaching seemed unthinkable, but this I did. Having been accepted as a candidate for the ministry I found myself in the Theological College of the Presbyterian Church of Wales at Aberystwyth. It was there, through the hand of God bearing heavily upon me showing me my spiritual poverty, and the faithful witness of some of the fine young men, that I sought the Lord in earnest and he had mercy upon me. Everything became alive and new. The verses which as children we had to recite in front of the congregation each Sabbath day, and those we learned for our Sunday School lessons, all became alive to me. The catechism became real – nothing from my religious background was wasted. But most thrilling of all, I had a message to preach. The actual event happened when I was on my own, staying in the preacher's room at a chapel house on a Saturday night. As I looked over my messages for the services on the next day, the Lord came to me and has not left me since. Dreams of popularity went out of the window, but peace and reality came in. Later I can remember pinning on the wall of my study this verse,

All that I am He made me,
All that I have He gave me,
And all that I ever hope to be
Jesus alone can do for me.

It was settled – the great transaction was done. Only a few days previously I had decided to return to my old profession because I felt that I had nothing to offer as a minister, and really nothing to say. Now there was plenty to say in the presentation of the gospel of our Lord and Saviour Jesus Christ. The quest was at an end but the pursuit of God and the pilgrimage of grace had begun. A verse that became very real to me at that time was Nahum 1:7: 'The Lord is good, a strong hold in the day of trouble; and he knoweth them that trust in him' (AV).

A partnership of service
During my stay at Aberystwyth I met my future wife who then was engaged in Christian work. She served as what was termed a 'sister of the people' with the Presbyterian Church of Wales.

120

Her work was on a large housing estate, visiting, witnessing, holding large meetings for children and so on. We married and a life-long partnership of service began.

My first church was in a Welsh mining town. The chapel was naturally Welsh speaking and I served the Lord there for three years. Then I went to the most beautiful village imaginable in the green hills of west Wales. It was completely different but a most blessed place. In both churches I found that it was the now ageing revival people – 'the children of the revival', as they were called – who were a great comfort and support. Incidentally, in a branch chapel of my first church I met the first convert of the 1904 revival, and that was the sister of Evan Roberts, the young man so mightily used by God at that time. I can say without doubt that the converts of that revival were faithful all through their lives and were a benediction to the churches they attended.

Quite unexpectedly an invitation came to preach at a church in Cardiff, which is my present location. I had no intention of leaving the place I loved so much and, furthermore, I had only preached in English about half a dozen times. That was a great difficulty, especially in praying when I had no notes to follow. However, I went there and somehow from the beginning I knew in my heart it was the place I should be. The guidance, which normally I find a great problem, was incredibly clear. There was no possible way that I could not submit to the will of God. My farewell meeting was a very emotional and extremely sad occasion, especially as the church had only had three ministers before me, each serving for forty years. Their ministries spanned a hundred and twenty years, and here was I leaving after a mere four! Although I loved my people deeply, a clear call is a clear call and there was no question of disobedience.

Then began my work in Cardiff, and I soon realised that I had so much to learn. I immersed myself in endless activity – visiting, seeking new contacts, witnessing, running campaigns in nearby towns, until it seemed as if I had taken the responsibility for every soul in Cardiff. The burden was too heavy for me, and in any case I can see now that the battle is not ours but the Lord's. Finally there came a Saturday evening after the young people's meeting in our home had just finished. It was a strange feeling. I moved one of the chairs and found it too heavy for me. Later, when my wife had gone to bed, the phone rang and even that seemed difficult as I lifted the receiver. Somehow I got upstairs, but within a few hours I felt as if my breathing had stopped. Then it seemed to relax for a while before it would seize up again. By this time a doctor had been called, and then an ambulance arrived. I did not know what was happening, and apparently I responded to nothing around me. It is a strange experience to hover between life and death, with eternity virtually only a breath away.

Daily grace for daily need

I was seriously ill, and this illness was to last for fifteen years – although at that particular moment all the signs were that both the illness and my life would soon end. Eventually I discovered that it was a form of severe asthma (*status asthmaticus*), episodes of which at that time were especially difficult to treat. The pattern of life changed for the whole family, making the present and the future so uncertain. Yet through it all the Lord drew near in so many special ways, giving grace for each day and courage to go on. I had always wanted to write a hymn but there was no hope of this because I could not make the words rhyme or fit thoughts into such compact expression. Yet as I came round into consciousness after that first of so many similar attacks which were to follow, I somehow jotted a few words down. They were later looked at by a friend who called it a hymn:

I saw a new vision of Jesus,
A view I'd not seen here before,
Beholding in glory so wondrous
With beauty I had to adore.
I stood on the shores of my weakness,
And gazed at the brink of such fear;
'Twas then that I saw Him in newness,
Regarding Him fair and so dear.

My Saviour will never forsake me,
Unveiling His merciful face,
His presence and promise almighty,
Redeeming His loved ones by grace.
In shades of the valley's dark terror,
Where hell and its horror hold sway,
My Jesus will reach out in power,
And save me by His only way.

For yonder a light shines eternal,
Which spreads through the valley of gloom;
Lord Jesus, resplendent and regal,
Drives fear far away from the tomb.
Our God is the end of the journey,
His pleasant and glorious domain;
For there are the children of mercy,
Who praise Him for Calvary's pain.

The Lord graciously allowed me to preach but, on the first Sunday when I returned, as I gave out my text it was as if all my faculties refused to function. The congregation sang a hymn, and I wondered as I sat there, if I would ever preach again. I got up and, enabled by him, preached the usual length of sermon for forty to forty-five minutes. Strangely the text was from Daniel 5:23 (AV): 'The God in whose hand thy breath is.'

Expectations far exceeded

Over the next five years daily injections and two visits each week to the consultant became routine. At one time I had an appointment in London to see a very kind specialist and he confirmed that it was apparent that my time was short. My wife and I went to a nearby café for a cup of tea and decided to live for the Lord as best we could while life lasted, and we had peace. Movement was very difficult for me and any exertion was well-nigh impossible, but my consultant amazed me by saying, 'I will keep you going in that pulpit for as long as I can!' The problems that arose can be imagined, especially when I went away from the security of my medical care. For example, I was anxious for the children to enjoy life as normally as others but going on holiday became a nightmare. In all these circumstances however, I can only testify to the goodness of God.

Meanwhile, without my frenzied efforts and activities, the church where I ministered grew – and I virtually stood back and watched it happen. There was no possibility that I could say these were my achievements since all my strength was taken up in keeping alive. There were frequent periods in various hospitals, but in all this my wife and I quietly accepted our circumstances. I had no reason to complain. I had a kind and patient church, a lovely family, and I could still preach. Often, however, the pulpit steps seemed like a mountain to climb – but I got there.

The years passed by and my particular condition became a way of life that I never expected to change. It is true that we can 'rejoice in the Lord' (Habakkuk 3:18, AV), and that 'as thy days, so shall thy strength be' (Deuteronomy 33:25, AV). The nights were long and the days, I suppose, were laborious, but the abnormal becomes normal and our limitations become our usual sphere of life. I learned to live from where I was and found so much in just resting in the Lord, comforted by verses such as 'Be still, and know that I am God' (Psalm 46:10, AV). There is no greater contentment than being content in the Lord, the circumstances seem to become incidental. The apostle Paul wrote: 'I have learned, in whatsoever state I am, therewith to be content' (Philippians 4:11, AV). One writer has described Christian contentment as a rare jewel, and if he meant by rare that it was exceedingly delightful and to be desired, then I am sure he was right.

Quiet healing

There followed, quite unexpectedly, a change in my condition as I found myself in a very low state in the mornings. This puzzled me because I have never been inclined to feeling discouraged or despairing, although I can fully understand how many can. To me, it was a new and unwelcome experience. It was at that time that I was invited to take part in the opening of a new church building, when the sermon in the main afternoon service was to be preached by the late Dr Martyn Lloyd-Jones and I was asked to preach in the evening. After the services he spoke to me and asked me what was troubling me, since he had noted despair in my expression. While he felt that it was understandable, he was naturally concerned, but I told him that I could give no reason or explanation whatsoever. He decided that it was a matter for prayer and we went into the ministerial vestry together. Dr Lloyd-Jones, who was convinced that this was a spiritual attack and that we should resist the devil, then prayed to this end. Afterwards I remarked that the atmosphere in the room was striking, as if it was as gentle as velvet. 'It is the Lord's presence,' was his quiet reply. He did not pray for healing specifically, as so many kind and thoughtful people had urged in one way or another in the past.

On the way home that night I felt remarkably well and I commented to my companion that my father always seemed to feel well the day before he developed some illness or other. I feared that this might be true of myself but I was proved to be wrong. In fact, this well-being lasted not only emotionally, but physically as well. At first I did not notice the change because I was so used to living within limitations, but it was not very long before I began to realise that more had happened in that prayer time in that little room than I had appreciated. Steadily the medication for my complaint was lessened and then dropped altogether. Dr Lloyd-Jones believed that it was an example of instantaneous healing, and the incident was mentioned in his biography.

Although I welcomed the new-found health, I was reluctant to make any claims of healing since I was anxious not to bring any discredit upon the gospel. In recent times so many unwise claims have been made that perhaps I was overcautious. It was not due to ingratitude on my part, but rather a desire to maintain the integrity of the gospel and not to cause any discredit on our Saviour's name. My reply to all who noticed the change was, 'Hitherto hath the Lord helped us' (1 Samuel 7:12, AV). Nevertheless the weeks became months, and the months years, and there was no further relapse, indeed my excellent health and strength continued.

Bonus years

By this time my children had grown up and they had to get used to this new father. As the years have passed by I began to call them my bonus years, and now it is as if I had never been ill. The memory of such weakness quickly fades when it is replaced by a full, active life. The day I preached on that never-to-be-forgotten occasion in my life, a tree was planted – just a tiny, frail thing, but today it is a joy to behold in all its beautiful full-grown splendour. That tree is a constant reminder to me of the goodness of the Lord. Almost twenty years have gone by, and I have reached the age of promise. No one, least of all myself, would have believed this to be possible. Last year we celebrated our ruby wedding and we had a photograph taken of my wife and me with our three children and their partners and eight grand-children. When I see it I often pause and give thanks to the One who does all things well.

At the same time I would add that contentment is not found in health or ill-health, in weakness or in strength, but in the Lord himself. Amy Carmichael said, 'In acceptance lieth peace.' That peace is from God alone and is to be cherished.

How good is the God we adore,
Our faithful, unchangeable Friend,
His love is as great as His power,
And knows neither measure nor end!

'Tis Jesus, the First and the Last,
Whose Spirit shall guide us safe home;
We'll praise Him for all that is past,
And trust him for all that's to come.

(Joseph Hart)

9

ESMÉ DUNCAN

For most of my life I have felt a certain contentment about being single. I attended an all-girls' school, but enjoyed teenage friendship with boys in dancing lessons, inter-school events and in Rubislaw Church of Scotland Youth Fellowship in my home town of Aberdeen. Two friendships were important in my late teens, the second was fairly serious on his part, but I was not ready for that. From the age of eleven I was certain my vocation was teaching and, when this was confirmed after I became a Christian at nineteen, I did not look for the years immediately ahead to include marriage and children. Being single would, I felt, leave me free to respond to God's leading.

Having been brought up in a faithful church-going family I don't remember a time when God was not important to me, but it was through Scripture Union that I met people who seemed to know Jesus as a real Person. About to leave school, I joined the Church and took my vows easily. But later, in a service in Pitlochry, the words of Jesus: 'No-one who puts his hand to the plough and looks back is fit for service in the Kingdom of God'

(Luke 9:62), challenged me to face the fact that my following him was inconsistent and my fate was to be cut off from the Kingdom of God. As I loved God, and the prospect of separation from him was unthinkable, I grasped the counsel of a friend to invite Jesus into my life, and, in August 1960, entered new life as a Christian.

My father died suddenly at the age of 58. I was in my final year of teacher training, and had thought of applying for a job in Stirlingshire where I had some close friends and would be nearer Glasgow and Edinburgh where Scripture Union was strong. While my mother was not one to stand in my way, I knew I could not be happy leaving her. My plans had to be set aside for the immediate future. I applied to the City of Aberdeen for a job and was appointed to one of its toughest schools. But God had other ideas, and, in August 1964, I started my chosen career as an assistant teacher of English and Religious Education in Aberdeen High School for Girls, where I had been a pupil since the age of nine. Knowing that I am a 'sticker', my sister declared that she could imagine me retiring some forty years later from that same school!

Towards the end of my twenties I explored possible moves. Having no marriage partner to consider, and confident that my mother was coping well with widowhood, I pushed doors to see what would happen. None opened and I continued teaching, finding in it happiness and fulfilment. But the Lord had other plans for me.

God leads the way

'That would be a good job for you, Esmé.' It was June 1969, and members of the Aberdeen Scripture Union Committee and Prayer Group were discussing the need for a new East of Scotland Staff Worker, following the illness and resignation of Sheila Kilpatrick. Laughter echoed round the room, the loudest from me. Nothing seemed less likely! Yet this was God's call. But, like Samuel, I needed to hear his voice a further two times over the following summer before I recognised it.

Leaving home in April 1970 to be based in Edinburgh was a challenge for me, but a wrench for my mother. She in no way held me back, even months later when she suffered a heart attack and was diagnosed as having angina. Her anxieties over my decision were entirely for me. I was giving up a very good job in a prestigious school for a calling which might be a blind alley. But as she saw how I adapted to my new role, thrilled by the challenge of assuming responsibility for SU work in the East of Scotland from the Moray Coast to the Borders, she relaxed and was happy for me. As the years passed, she welcomed and grew to love the colleagues and new friends whom I brought home. She came to mean a lot to them too.

During my years in SU field work it was a great advantage being single. I was free to travel widely and found it easy to get accommodation. Many of the teachers and others with whom I forged friendships entrusted me with a key and I came and went over the period of my visits, spending enough time with them to let friendship develop and fellowship become richer, but allowing them to continue without the burden of entertaining me. My home base, first in Edinburgh with Billie Smith, and then later with Myra Wallace and then Alma Johnstone in Scone, was organised on similar lines.

One disadvantage of being single was that it was too easy to let work dominate my life. Having no-one else to consider, I could, and sometimes did, work all day every day for weeks on end. It was not always easy to know what was work. The defining lines between it and just living were hazy or non-existent, and, since I loved practically every aspect of my job – was much of it not what I had eagerly devoted my spare time to in my teaching days? – I just got on with it. I was constantly thrilled by the privilege of what I was doing.

Hard times ahead

Then the problems began, and it was hard to be single. My mother died suddenly, while I was leading a summer camp at Seamill. My aunt's phone call came through during a lunchtime – 'Esmé, I have to tell you, your mother's dead.' Somehow I imagined that I would be at home when this happened. On some previous occasions I had gone through to her bedroom in the morning, half expecting that her increasingly precarious hold on life had slipped from her grasp, but each time she rallied. Her quality of life had been poor for a while. She, whom I vividly remembered from childhood days walking at a rate I found hard to equal, needed frequent rests on garden walls on her return from the nearby shops.

I was not, of course, completely on my own. My sister Jenny and I had not been close in childhood and teenage years. Like many siblings only eighteen months apart we lived in a state of enmity. But, in adult life, circumstances drew us together and we were slowly becoming good friends. Now our only real barrier was the five hundred miles between Aberdeen and her home in Hertfordshire. How grateful I was that my aunt who had told me of my mother's death lived with her sister not far from me. She had returned to Aberdeen, as a widow, in the early eighties when her sister retired. They lovingly supported my mother when I was away from home, now they supported me.

Years before, from her own experience, Billie had shared things which I found to be true as my life unfolded, among them the particular trauma for the single person of the death of her second parent. How accurate Billie's description had been. No longer could I be confident that I rated first in the life of another. I had close friends to whom I could turn, but they had their families. Single friends had responsibilities for parents or they lived at a distance. Jenny was far away and she had her own life and circle of friends. While we obviously shared our loss, I was on my own when she returned home.

Who am I?

My mother's death forced me to reassess my own identity. As far as my status as a Christian was concerned, nothing had changed, and I found great comfort in the presence of the God of all comfort, and in the answered prayers of my many friends. But the focus of human relationships was different, and I had to take steps which would help to determine the course of my life.

I have mentioned my aunt, but I had some other relatives too. My mother also had a number of close friends, and I needed to make decisions about each of these relationships. My share in them had largely been second-hand; if they were to continue, I had to take some initiative. I made mistakes and fear that some of my mother's friends may have felt abandoned. But, as the years passed, I have been able to visit some and to maintain contact with others by adding them to the long list of those who receive an update of my news each Christmas.

Had I been married, I feel sure that the value of – and responsibility for – these relationships might not have seemed so great. And I doubt whether I could have set aside the time for them. As one grows older the things of the past appear to take on a new importance, or perhaps one discovers the importance they always had.

To the friends of my mother, I was Elsie's daughter. To my own friends, I was the person they knew and shared experiences with; to my colleagues and supporters in SU, I was one who worked hard, thoroughly committed to the work to which God had called me. And to myself, I was.... Here I stumbled, facing a question which I suddenly could not answer. At the time I did not realise what was going on inside me. All I knew was the certainties of the past were out of reach, and the present and the future were so, so uncertain.

If I had realised what was happening, and found someone with whom I could have shared my feelings, perhaps things might have turned out very differently. One of my SU colleagues suggested that I get in touch with an SU supporter who is a doctor, but I lacked the confidence to approach her. It became increasingly hard even to pray about my problems. What someone called 'that dratted evangelical conscience' kept telling me I should have the resources in my faith to enable me to overcome. But I could not grasp them. I came away from church feeling miserable, guilty, confused; the words of Scripture, hymns and sermons confirming my inability to help myself or to find help in what I had believed for so long. Close friends were too close to discuss properly what I most needed to talk about – had I been able to put it into words. Or they were so occupied with their own concerns that they, and I, felt frustrated. A bitterness crept in as I became more and more unhappy.

Part of the answer lay in an appreciation of the importance of arithmetic! I was in my mid-forties, a natural time of change which brings its own difficulties to everyone. Add to that my mother's death (with the unlooked-for added grieving for my father whose death I had not known how to cope with at the time) when my stress level was already too high. While enjoying living on my own, I always had home to return to – the home in which I had been born. But, knowing that it made no sense to retain a house built in the late thirties and now requiring work done and money spent – and it was too large for one – I was seeking a flat. That quest took eight months, at the end of which I put my home on the market. Showing prospective buyers round brought back long forgotten memories! Selling removed yet another foundation: how insecure could I make myself?

Where do I go from here?

But I ploughed on. I believed I had been led to Peterculter, on the Deeside edge of Aberdeen, and within three weeks of buying a flat there, the family home was sold. More changes were afoot. I was about to leave SU, having served for five years followed by a year's 'sabbatical' back in the classroom. Two consecutive periods of five years were coming to an end and I was convinced that, just as certainly as God had called me into the work, he was calling me out of it. Although I was tired *in* the work, I most certainly was not tired *of* the work.

Some changes bring a lightening of spirit. New challenges lay ahead and I was sure that God was in control. Amazed and distressed, however, I watched as three former SU colleagues faced unemployment or part-time working. But within three months I not only had a job, but found myself in a promoted post – Assistant Principal Teacher of Religious Education in Kemnay Academy. Incredibly, I found that two of my new colleagues lived within a few hundred yards of me allowing us to travel the thirty mile round trip to school together. Having driven thousands of miles in SU field work with only thoughts and prayers, or the radio, for company, it took time to adjust to starting the day with two others, both of whom were married.

They usually had a great deal to say, offloading

the problems of work and home, while I sat mostly in silence. When only one was present I would contribute a little, but usually in response to what the other had said. There was much that I could have spoken of: I found huge difficulties in returning to the classroom, and teenage youngsters are not known for giving the R E teacher an easy time. Much more than that, although I failed completely to realise it, the stress brought about by all the changes was battering me into a state of desperation. I felt as if I was constantly climbing a mountain, usually on my hands and knees. It seemed I would make a little progress and then something, or someone, would push me back. And when, unknown to them, that push came from a close friend or a word in a Christian context, the unhappiness which I felt was all the greater. It seemed that even those who loved me most were failing me.

The ironic thing about the journeys home from school was that, because my colleagues found satisfaction in offloading their problems, when their husbands came in they were able to get on with their evenings together. But I took my problems home with me, home where there was no-one to share them. I went over and over them in my mind, or sometimes aloud, but they did not go away. How I needed someone to talk to. There was, of course, the telephone, but sharing at depth with someone who may be preoccupied with what was going on around them just increased my frustration.

Alone and lonely

Being single had become almost too hard to bear. I became increasingly lonely and would often return from school or from an evening meeting only to sit in the car for a long time in tears, or go into my flat and wander round aimlessly, still with my jacket on, for an hour or more. On the whole, I hid my unhappiness.

Eventually, it could be hidden no longer, and on one December Monday I was encouraged to sort out some work for my classes and take the rest of the week off work. What a relief to be free for a few days from one source of the stress I was experiencing! In the end, I was off until mid January. My doctor helped me understand something of what was going on, and particularly encouraged me not to feel in any sense a failure.

I spent that New Year, as I usually did, at an SU Houseparty, among many friends most of whom are single. Humanly speaking I was surrounded by all the strength and empathy I needed. But human help was of little help. As the year ended and the new year began at the Watchnight Service in Pitlochry Baptist Church, I slipped away from the happy celebrations.

God is faithful: help was at hand. I am in the habit of reading each morning from *Daily Light*, and the verse leapt from the page, speaking powerfully: 'Forgetting what is behind ... I press on towards the goal to win the prize for which God has called me heavenwards in Christ Jesus' (Philippians 3:13-14). There and then God's Holy Spirit filled me with his strength; the Encourager encouraged me, and I began to look forward. There was a long way to go, but things have never been so bad again.

Mungo

Always having been a dog lover I had thought that my first acquisition on retirement would be a dog. But I realised during my weeks of absence from school that the dog-shaped space in my life needed to be filled sooner than that. On my return from Pitlochry, I knocked at the door of the Cat and Dog Home. 'We only have six dogs, no bitches,' the assistant apologised. It was a dog I wanted: I had already decided to call him Mungo. And there he was, six months old, a pathetic abandoned Labrador/collie cross, picked up by the dog warden and shivering in the kennel in his loneliness. 'I'll take him.' The decision was easy: he needed love and I desperately wanted something to love. It was only later that I began to realise how much love he was capable of giving in return – and I believe that the One who sees the sparrow fall was watching over that puppy. It is impossible to measure how much Mungo contributed towards my recovery.

More was to follow. My caring GP showed real perception. Having seen him regularly until early summer he asked me to return in the autumn. With my medical notes in front of him, he enquired if I had ever heard of SAD – *Seasonal Affective Disorder* – a syndrome which affects many people as winter approaches and days shorten, making them unhappy and depressed. It was clear that my worst periods were between November and mid-February. For years I had found Christmas hard to cope with, and had attributed the slight turn for the better towards the end of February to the passing of the anniversary of my father's death. As I learned more about SAD, and thought back over many years, I could picture myself carrying a rucksack into which, around early October, sand began to be poured, until in December I was struggling under its weight. Towards the end of February a tiny hole was bored in the rucksack out of which the sand trickled until, by June, it was empty. But I was never able to put the rucksack down and, as the effect was cumulative, the autumn was clouded with the anticipation of the spoiling effect of the sand to come.

My doctor offered me the chance to take part in trials of a drug being tested on patients with SAD. I could have been given a placebo, my doctor would not have known as the trials were conducted double blind, but I was not. The effect was amazing. By the time the trials ended and the medication stopped, I was a new person. The rucksack was discarded and, six years on, it has not been replaced. With what gratitude I describe that release.

A new day dawns

Having come through deep waters, I can once more testify to finding that being single is a state which offers positive contentment and special opportunities. I have learned to seek openings to share and talk through problems before they grow. My appreciation of family members who are still around me and particularly the friendship of my sister, although we are very different, has increased greatly. And I count it a privilege when my experience helps me to empathise with others who pass through difficult times.

The last six years have, of course, held their share of problems, but God has continued to enable and guide. They have held their challenges too. Early retirement coincided with the final part of training as a Reader in the Church of Scotland. I anticipate being used in remote areas when the need arises as, being single, I am free to be away from home for longish periods. And I look forward to seeing where God will send me. Here I am, Lord...

I expect I will, from time to time, have to

prepare and conduct services specifically advertised as being for those of all ages, and, where possible, I shall call these ALL AGE SERVICES, remembering how the use of the term FAMILY SERVICE only heightened my feelings of loneliness. The Christian Family is a reality, but I wonder if single people, whether never married, widowed or single by any other circumstance, feel completely assured that they are seen as brothers, sisters, aunts, uncles, grandparents and so on, to those who are present in their real families. ALL AGE reaches out and warmly welcomes everyone in. If those who are alone cannot find inclusion in the fellowship of saints, they are lonely indeed.

10

JONATHAN LAMB

Living with a mild disability from early childhood eventually becomes normal. You don't perceive yourself to be different from others; your expectations of life are similar; and eventually your coping mechanisms become so much second nature that it is almost a surprise when people regard you as disabled. So much so, that I confess I feel something of a fraud contributing to a book some of whose other contributors have passed through far more demanding circumstances than I have.

But we each have a unique personality and Christian calling. The interface between our personality, our experience of life, and the impact of God's grace, whilst different for each one of us, also highlights common themes which can strengthen and encourage God's people in their varied circumstances. Perhaps some elements of my own experience will help others, and it is in this spirit that I offer this brief account of my story.

Formative influences

Leaving school at the age of twelve, my father began his working life helping the local milkman in north London. He then drove London buses for many years. We lived in a small terraced house owned by the London Borough of Barnet. Nothing about my parents' life could be described as lavish or pretentious. But it would be hard to over-cstimate the influence of my father on my own world view and spiritual growth. His gentle and humble spirit, his willingness to serve others, his warm spirituality, and even his bright eyes and genuine smile, all impacted me early in life. He gave his energies to caring for us and to building up a small church in our town.

Two events in my early childhood stand out as particularly vivid memories in what was otherwise an uneventful and relatively normal upbringing. In 1956 an evangelist came to our small church, where my father ran a children's club each Monday evening. Although I was only five years old, I joined the crowd of older children - one of the few perks of having a father leading the group. At the end of a simple presentation, the visiting evangelist invited any who wished to become Christians to come to the front. A number of children shuffled forward, and I was amongst them. Noticing I was considerably smaller than the rest, the evangelist placed his hand on my head, turned me round, and sent me back to my seat.

I don't carry any emotional scars – at least not from that experience! It was understandable on his part, fearful of an unthinking response and of inappropriate peer pressure on an impressionable young child. But my response to the Christian message was real enough. I remember one over-riding conviction: I needed to be forgiven. So when we returned home, my father, who had witnessed the events during the appeal, encouraged me to pray with him that night if I genuinely did want to become a member of God's family. And so I did. Based on a child-like understanding of Jesus' death for me, I asked to be forgiven. So began a journey of faith and commitment that has lasted 40 years.

The second event occurred only a matter of months later. One morning I stepped out of bed and my legs collapsed beneath me. I remember laughing about it, despite the concerned look on my parents' faces, for every time I tried to stand my legs buckled underneath me. Investigations eventually revealed that I was a victim of what turned out to be London's final wave of polio. I had recently been in hospital for the removal of my tonsils (kept proudly, like tropical fish, in some strange coloured liquid by my bedside), and this left me susceptible to infection. Within a matter of days both arms and both legs were affected.

Human and divine compassion

Being a parent now I can imagine something of the turmoil my parents must have experienced. But, throughout my childhood, I do not have a single memory of their frustration with me, their anger at God, or any expression of bewilderment on their part. The environment in which I was brought up was nothing other than totally supportive and compassionate. I was carried by my father up and down hills on family walks, encouraged to throw myself into as many activities as possible, and above all, to keep on trusting God. Such recollection has provoked me to attempt a similar steady consistency with my own children, through the inevitable ups and downs of childhood and adolescence. The reaction of my parents is only a pale reflection of God's compassionate understanding for his children. Yet it is often through such human examples that we come to understand more fully the divine concern for our well-being.

I have a few recollections of emotional difficulty. First, not wanting to stay in hospital for the first of several operations. I frequently appealed to my parents that one of them should move to live in the ward with me. The strange noises and eerie light of the night-time remain as vivid memories, but I soon became a part of the hospital community and quite enjoyed moving around at breakneck speed in a hospital wheelchair.

The second difficulty occurred when I eventually realized, at age 10 or 11, that I would not grow out of the condition, but would have the disability for the rest of my life. As I moved into my early teens this became more difficult to come to terms with. It was only years later that I discovered that many people around the world had been praying for my recovery. The Christian community to which we belonged was small, but nearly always Christians are well networked! My parents felt that, although I was not healed completely, perhaps my subsequent spiritual growth was the result of the prayers of God's people in different parts of the world.

By the age of 11 it was clear I would never run again. My right arm and left leg showed signs of positive recovery; but my right leg in particular was extremely weak (the muscle would never recover). This was a frustration in the playground of Underhill Primary School! But I had an appallingly stubborn insistence that I would take part in everything I could with as much energy as I had at my disposal. Wise and imaginative PE masters at each school I attended found ways of harnessing that energy. After various surgical attempts to encourage my right leg to adapt, I entered my teens with no serious disability other than a much weaker and shorter right leg, which necessitated wearing a surgical shoe and using a walking stick.

Simple things became an emotional rather than a physical challenge. Keeping pace on school geography field courses, is an example, with the embarrassment of being carried down Cader Idris by the Geography master; or finding trousers that would cover what seemed to me to be an unsightly shoe; or being unable to wear trendy sports shoes. It is surprising how such apparently insignificant matters impacted my desire to find acceptance amongst teenage friends. But by God's grace, other areas of my life enabled me to connect with friends in unexpected ways, whether in music, social programmes, Christian activity, or sports requiring less mobility such as table tennis. My university days were similar: immediate involvement with the Christian Union resulted in many opportunities for friendships and a wide range of activity which meant my disability gradually receded into the background.

On the road
It is something of an irony to a number of my friends that, for someone with mobility problems, so much of my life should have been taken up with travelling. For the past 20 years my work – with the Universities and Colleges Christian Fellowship, then in church-based ministry, and then with the International Fellowship of Evangelical Students – has taken me all over the British Isles, to most countries of Europe, and to

parts of the former USSR, North America and Africa. Other friends have suggested that this is part of God's grace, providing a form of compensation for those areas of life which have been closed to me. If that is the case, it is an expression of God's wonderful generosity, for the small losses I might have endured seem to be very little compared to the privileges of my present work.

Inevitably, travel has its stresses and strains, but the coping mechanisms devised by most people with disabilities mean that travel is now a normal and relatively easy part of my life. On the road I notice that disability is another opportunity for engaging in conversation with others. It is quite common for people to offer help (most particularly in Eastern Europe), and people regularly ask about both my job and the reason for the walking stick. Such concern affords natural opportunities for sensitive Christian witness.

Intriguingly, I am rarely asked about my disability by Christians. Non-Christians seem to be much more up-front, perhaps less embarrassed, but I am not entirely sure how to analyse this difference. Are Christians better adjusted, able to accept people as they are, without feeling the need to enquire? Perhaps. Is this part of being in the same family? My wife and children, for example, accept my circumstances entirely naturally, with the ideal balance of understanding and support alongside good humour and the necessary gentle mockery from time to time, which helps me avoid any form of self pity and keeps things in proportion. Self pity is destructive of our capacity to love, and we nearly always need others to help us refocus.

On the other hand, it is often quite refreshing when non-Christians come out with it in a very direct manner and, as I have implied, this opens the door for useful discussion. So I usually make a point, when meeting someone with an obvious handicap, to be sensitive in discussion, not interrogating inappropriately but, where it is natural and comfortable for the person concerned, asking them to tell me something of their story. Whether the person is a Christian or not, this nearly always leads us to compare notes along the way, and draws us together.

Independence and empathy
There is within my experience something of a paradox with which others might identify. Disabled people like myself can be notoriously independent. We have fierce reactions when asked 'does he take sugar?'; we take on extraordinarily zany projects such as sponsored wheelchair journeys from Land's End to John O'Groats. This is often because we have to be independent. The alternative might mean giving up the struggle to do something significant – for some people, even

giving up on life itself. We develop a determination, perhaps even a fool-hardiness, gritting our teeth with a resolve to achieve our goal. All of this is understandable and, when placed at God's disposal, can be very productive.

On the other hand – and here lies the paradox – we are often people who, through the experience of difficulty, also develop an empathy and pastoral concern, seeing our need to trust other people and benefit from true community. It is not always easy for us independent types to accept help, of course, and this has from time to time been a hard lesson for me to learn. Cultivating the willingness to receive is a fundamental need for all Christians, able-bodied or otherwise, for the entire Christian faith is built around God's grace. I look upon my own experience of handicap as a regular reminder of the need to learn to receive.

Whenever assistance is offered, even for those things which I know are well within my abilities to achieve unaided, I try to respond with acceptance and gratitude. It is frequently personal pride which provokes the independent reaction that insists I can manage. So these themes belong together: the importance of sustained determination, personal discipline, the refusal to give up (all of which I hope are fed by God's grace and his gift of inward strength); coupled with the importance of dependence on others, a humble attitude that does not dismiss help as patronising but is thankful for help and for the humanity and compassion which lie behind it.

Identity and security

For many of us, the question of self worth also lies behind our reactions in these areas. Contemporary culture stresses image the whole time. Our expectations of the good life are fed by media images of beautiful bodies and designer clothes. Plastic surgery is a growing industry, helping us resolve problems associated with too large a nose or too small a bust. Ultimately we come to measure our sense of self worth by the superficial standards set by the consumer society. Our weight, our hair loss, our health and fitness, our lifestyle – each becomes significant in our desire to be accepted.

It is surprising how ingrained this has become, even for us Christians. In such a culture we need to find our identity as persons in the God who made us and who knows every detail of the circumstances through which we are passing. It took me several years, after the innocent and naive years of childhood, to cope with the stares and occasional pointed finger when I entered a swimming pool. Part of this was coming to terms with myself through the inevitable transitions of adolescence; but part of it was learning to accept my disability and not be insecure about who I was, or where my identity and acceptance truly lay.

My tactics varied when I was younger: sometimes I was angry that people should stare, and would reply with a long cold stare in return. Sometimes I couldn't cope with being the object of such attention, and kept my eyes on the ground for as long as possible. Even now I feel uncomfortable, but have decided that the most useful response is to smile back.

Nowadays social culture has changed somewhat. I write these words in an Oxford café, sitting opposite a girl with fluorescent orange hair, and no one bats an eyelid. This is partly because of the unusual café society in the student quarter of town; but it is also part of the cultural shift, which increasingly accepts people of all shapes and sizes, colours and creeds. There is an aspect of such tolerance which we Christians would not support; but there is also a welcome side, which allows people to be what they are, including the disabled. But at a far deeper level the issue remains: where does my sense of identity, self worth, and security come from? In today's youth culture this remains one of the most pressing issues. It provides an evangelistic opportunity to be grasped by those who know that their life, their personhood and their destiny are tied to their relationship with the living Lord Jesus.

When I am weak

There are several other theological themes which my simple experience of disability have illuminated. The first is Paul's paradox of strength in weakness. His great exposition of this theme appears in 2 Corinthians, where he highlights that, since God's power was displayed through the apparent weakness of the crucified Jesus, so God's power will be seen best in the weakness of those who carry that gospel message. In Paul's case this was borne out through the demands of his Christian ministry which clearly brought him close to death. But the principle has been enormously helpful to me in coping with aspects of physical weakness too. It is the testimony of Christians through the centuries, eloquently expressed by others in this book, that our human weakness encourages us to be far more dependent on the Lord than we might otherwise have been. As Jim Packer wisely observes in his book *Knowing God*: 'This is the ultimate reason, from our standpoint, why God fills our lives with troubles and perplexities of one sort or another – it is to ensure that we shall learn to hold him fast.'

My own small infirmity has encouraged me to be more deliberate in looking for God's hand in situations of trial. And where his hand seems invisible, or the event seems to lack meaning, I seek to learn to trust him more fully. On the basis of past evidence, he knows what he is doing. The real tragedy of suffering, as Mary Craig observes in her moving book *Blessings*, is the wasted opportunity. We can see ourselves 'as the ill-used victims of outrageous fate', or we can grasp the opportunity to learn more about ourselves, about God's ability to respond to our need, and as Mary Craig expresses it, 'grasp suffering by the throat and use it.'

Now and not yet

Secondly, I have come to appreciate the New Testament theme of 'now and not yet'. Let me relate this to the vexed question of healing. I have been in many contexts where leaders have appealed to people to come forward for prayer for healing. I frequently speak at conferences or Christian gatherings where people will offer to lay hands on me, and pray for healing. I know that this is always well motivated, even if at times the approach is a little insensitive. Over many years, from childhood onwards, people have prayed for my healing. Indeed, as a leader in church settings I have responded to requests from church members who have followed the clear instructions given by James, and I have prayed with them for their healing.

All of us would want to affirm God's ability to intervene and heal us; none of us should ever become cynical about its possibility. But I encounter many Christians who have been at the receiving end of well meaning people who imply that it is God's will that they should be healed, and who have therefore urged them to have more faith or to confess their sin. To such people – both the protagonists and their unfortunate victims – I have tried to present a simple apologetic for the biblical theme of 'now and not yet'. To put it another way: Paul's use of the idea of firstfruits is a helpful illustration of what we are to expect. It has helped me to be more relaxed about the issue of healing in my own life.

If God's Kingdom is here, we should expect to see signs of that Kingdom now; there should be some evidence of his powerful working – what we might call the firstfruits. And around the world, and in our own lives, we see the evidence. We rejoice with those who are healed, whether through the services of doctors (for this is part of God's healing grace) or through the exercise of a healing gift within the Christian community. But there is also a 'not yet'. The full experience of what it means to live in God's Kingdom, with all its wholeness, peace and restoration, is yet to come.

So it is wise to avoid both errors: either the error of suggesting that there is no fruit on the tree, or the error of suggesting that the tree must be full of fruit now. The Biblical concept of first-fruits is realistic: we expect some evidence of God's intervention, and pray in humble dependence on his wisdom and sovereignty. But we should not expect everything to be resolved now. Indeed, to try to live with such expectations is to miss the force of Paul's description of the gospel and Christian living, and the Lord's promise to him and to us: 'My grace is sufficient for you, for my power is made perfect in weakness' (2 Corinthians 12:9).

As Paul Tournier once observed, 'We are nearly always looking for an easy religion, easy to understand, and easy to follow, a religion with no mystery, no insoluble problems, no snags; a religion that would allow us to escape from our miserable human condition; a religion in which our contact with God spares us all strife, all uncertainty, all suffering and all doubt; in short, a religion without the cross.'

Sufficient for today
And finally, what about the future? I do not now mean the 'not yet' of heaven, but the immediate future between now and then. For scripture encourages us to face the unknown with hope and trust. This too has had to be a conscious decision as I have grown older. Some medics have predicted difficulties ahead. Back problems are likely. I have just been sent a fax from the British Polio Fellowship which reads, 'Many polio survivors are experiencing new and unexpected physical problems and we have information that

may help them to avoid long term damage to their health.' It would be foolish for me to ignore health warnings. But I know it would also be foolish to get caught in the trap of fearing for the future.

Our lives, short or long, healthy or disabled, are in God's hands. Jesus was right when he urged us to take no thought for the morrow. He was not suggesting irresponsible management of our lives or the evasion of wise precautionary measures; but he was encouraging us to trust the Creator and Redeemer, who loves us and has nothing but good purposes planned for us. That's why the healthiest attitude is surely – let's get on with the job. Tomorrow is God's business.

11

KATIE MORRISON

'Don't take your daughter home – she's not going to live.' That's what my mother was told when I was born forty five years ago. I was a 'blue baby', having been born with a restriction in the aorta, the main artery leading from the heart to the lungs. My mother, a Christian and a trained nurse, decided she would take me home and care for me as long as I lived. All these years later the fact that I am still here to tell this tale is testimony to my parents' love for me, to the fine medical care I have received, and especially to the goodness of God. He had a purpose for my life.

Looking back my childhood years seemed to be spent on the move, although it did not feel like it at the time. I suppose when there are five children in a family, as there were in ours – I was the second youngest – so much remained the same even if the place we lived in changed. From Zimbabwe we went to Kent, from Kent to Sussex, then back again, all before going to Wales aged thirteen. I found the move to Wales difficult, especially having to adapt to a co-educational school. Recognising my problem my parents persuaded the education authorities to allow me to return to Tonbridge Girls' Grammar School for two years to take my exams. The first year I stayed with one of my father's sisters and the second I lived in digs. From time to time I felt very homesick but found great comfort in attending the local church, praying, and writing long letters home to my mother.

Early lessons in the Christian faith

It was my mother who taught me my first spiritual truths. I have a clear memory of her taking me on to her knee after I had been involved in a row with my sisters, and explaining to me about Jesus and the cross. I can hear her words still. 'The cross stands for "I" crossed out.' I grew up believing that I must be good, work hard, not make a fuss and not be selfish. Teaching at church at that stage could be summed up as 'try to keep the Ten Commandments and the Sermon on the Mount and be a good girl and you'll go to heaven'. It was not until years later that I first heard the doctrines of grace and the need for repentance and faith in the Lord Jesus Christ. But even as a young girl away from home, God made me conscious of a spiritual need within myself. My letters home reflected this, I was sure my mother would understand.

In 1970 I went to Glasgow to study for a BA degree in Hotel and Catering Management at Strathclyde University. My mother came with me to help me find suitable accommodation and she was horrified by the state of the tenements and their stairwells or 'closes'. Eventually I booked in to the YWCA Hostel right in the middle of Glasgow and spent four happy terms there. In spite of the living conditions of many, I found the Glasgow people so friendly and hospitable, and I shall always have 'a soft spot' for them.

My spiritual search led me to the local Church of Scotland for my first experience of Presbyterianism. Liking it very much I would have continued there had I not been introduced to the Scottish Episcopal Church whose form of service was more familiar to me. I went early one Easter Sunday morning and was thrilled by the sunshine pouring in on a host of daffodils decorating the sanctuary. Deeply moved, and receptive to the story of the resurrection that was preached during the service, I knew I had found a home.

From then on I attended regularly and came to know the rector well. He held a youth Bible Study in his home once a week. I loved to go and benefited so much. That was where I first learned to recognise God's blessings and answers to prayer. The rector began each week by asking us to share how God had blessed us during the previous seven days. The first time he asked the question we were silent, unable to think of anything at all. But we soon learned to treasure up our blessings and share them with the rest of the group. 'Count your blessings name them one by one, Count your blessings see what God has done...' became a reality in my life.

Widening horizons

My brother, who had gone to Australia, wrote with the news that he was going to be married in December 1976. By then I was working in the Marketing Department of a large engineering company in Glasgow as Personal Secretary to the Director of Corporate Planning. But I was close to my brother and wanted to go to his wedding. There seemed to be three obstacles – I needed a work permit if I was going to stay for some time, I needed money for my fare, and what should I do about my well paid job? I prayed and God answered. The Australian Embassy gave me a work permit, my sister lent me the fare and my boss gave me a year's leave of absence. In my youthfulness I had made a bargain with God – if I got to Australia for a year I would commit myself to his service for the year. I know God has forgiven my youthful presumptuousness.

I left Britain in August and returned the following summer after my great adventure. Friends found me employment with the Church of Australia's Home Mission Board, working as a care assistant in a home for delinquent girls. While at the home, a student came to help and she was used by God to speak to my heart. Gaille had just finished Bible College and was alive with the Word of God. We had many long discussions lasting into the early hours of the morning, discussions in which I was always confronted with, 'But Katie, the Bible says ...!' How I wished I knew my Bible better. So it was that the seed of a hunger for the Word of God was planted.

The year which I had committed to the Lord was a time of learning about his faithfulness in answer to prayer. I discovered his sovereignty, was reassured by it, and I experienced his power, basking in God's willingness to provide for all my needs.

Returning to Scotland I found accommodation just across the road from another Episcopal Church on the south side of Glasgow. Friends there took me under their wing. They were voluntary helpers at a day centre for single homeless men. They also visited an alcohol rehabilitation centre one night a week to meet with the men there. For two years I went with them, learning about the work done in the name of Christ for those in need, and discovering something of the ravages of alcoholism. God was preparing a future for me, and preparing me to meet it.

Doctrines and debates

In 1978 the Lord led me away from my work and into full-time study at the Bible Training Institute in Glasgow. I loved studying the Bible and its doctrines – so much was new to me and each fresh truth was a source of excitement and wonder. Although I crammed almost two years work into one year I still had time to take part in lively debates in the common room! While at Bible College I committed myself fully to the Lord Jesus Christ. By then I had learned about sin and God's judgement and my need to be born again by the Holy Spirit. God was pleased to hear my prayer for forgiveness through Jesus Christ and to adopt me into the family of faith.

On completing my course I was appointed deputy officer in charge of a Christian alcohol rehabilitation centre in rural Scotland and, in the autumn of 1979, I went, fully persuaded that I was going to serve the Lord there. I was thrilled to find that we gave thanks to God before each meal, had a Bible reading with a brief exposition and prayer every morning and evening with the residents, and took them to church each Sunday. So eager was I to pass on the Good News that I became rather critical of others who did not share my enthusiasm. And the Lord has had to humble me from time to time over the years. I began attending the Free Church of Scotland where the preaching of God's Word did much to sustain my faith, and the kindness of God's people was greatly appreciated.

I worked hard and tried to live the Christian life day by day. The Lord poured out his blessings in many ways and in the course of my work I was privileged to see him restoring backslidden believers and bringing others to faith in Jesus Christ. Many visitors commented on the love and peace they experienced in the house. There were also disappointments, heartaches and conflicts. That was inevitable – we were people in need dealing with needy people.

A local house fellowship met once a week and the residents were invited. That meeting was a source of strength and encouragement to many, and a great help to me when the going got tough. I began to be wholly taken up with my job, working long hours over and above the call of duty, denying my own needs and sacrificing myself to my work. Becoming tired and angry, I felt lonely, unloved and unappreciated. Here I was caring for others, but who cared about me? Little wonder, then, that I burned out after ten years, exhausted by giving all the time and feeling I was not receiving much in return.

Happiness ... then a broken heart
During this period I met a man with whom I fell in love. We married in 1988, having known each other for two years. He seemed to be the man of my dreams and I was blissfully happy. At last someone loved me and cared for me. But that was not to last for long. My husband was a recovering alcoholic with deep emotional problems about

which I knew little. Our marriage fell apart very quickly. I was bewildered and afraid but God's word spoke to me: 'I have seen his ways, but I will heal him' (Isaiah 57:18). Where was God in all of this? I talked to Christian friends but did not find any help. I couldn't express my feelings. And, as I did not want to create a fuss, perhaps they thought I was coping. I could only hold on to the command: 'Have faith in God' (Mark 11:22), and I kept praying.

My father had been ill for a long time before he died in 1984. This unsettled me further. Should I move back to Kent to be with my mother? Then she had her legs amputated because of a circulation problem. She lived alone. What should I do?

Storm clouds gather

About the same time I learned that I could not continue working at the rehabilitation centre, and that I was unable, without a qualification, to gain promotion despite my years of experience. And then, a final shock and horror – my husband was arrested and charged with a very serious offence. He was found guilty and given a life sentence, to serve a minimum of six years 'punishment time'. I was stunned, but I loved him still and agreed to stand by him. I took my marriage vows seriously, and, remembering my promises were 'for better, for worse', I prayed that God would give me grace to keep them.

So I moved south to begin an MA in Social Work and to care for my mother. I was in shock and on 'automatic pilot'. Having left my home, job, friends, church and my adopted and much loved Scottish culture, I felt so alone. I could not tell anyone about my recent experiences or about my husband. Just coping became as much as I could achieve. At university I asked to see a counsellor and, after several weeks, someone gave me three quarters of an hour. Having opened my heart I was told I would have to wait a while for another appointment as there was a shortage of counsellors. Years later, I am still waiting. I became depressed and tearful, and at times very angry with others but I kept crying to God for help. What was wrong with me that, as a Christian, I was not full of joy and peace?

At that time I read several books about Christians experiencing difficult times and they always appeared to be surrounded by loving, caring friends. Their stories seemed to focus on the good things that were happening to them and the prayers that were answered, there was nothing of struggling with the kind of feelings and problems that were mine. Perhaps I read the wrong books. I felt so alone and unloved. Although I could make sense of nothing, I still believed in God and longed after him. I continued to pray and read my Bible each day, and the Holy Spirit often brought God's Word alive to me to give me encouragement and hope.

There were blessings, but all I could focus on was the depth of my own need. During my final year at university I was referred to another counsellor and she was, to some degree, helpful. Although I could talk to her our sessions did little to help me make sense of anything. I just seemed to be one big blob of pain and despair. But, in spite of it all, I finished my dissertation and gained my degree. I can only give God the glory for that, for without him I could never have done it.

On completing my studies I obtained employment as a probation officer and enjoyed the work, despite my misgivings about some parts of it. I still did not speak about my husband, but I visited him in jail three or four times a year. It was several hundred miles from my new home yet God provided for all my needs. I became friendly with a Christian family near the jail, and they welcomed me into their home and supported me throughout my visits which were often stressful and traumatic. What precious friends they have become. At last God had given me friends with whom I could share my feelings, and who understood and loved me.

Help at last

During an appraisal at work I explained that I felt lacking in some skills and my boss kindly agreed to allow me extra training on a one-to-one basis. As a visiting tutor, with whom I had been greatly impressed, had given me her card some time before, I decided to contact her for help. Our initial meeting was useful, and a foretaste of times together which would prove to be of immense value. How I thank God for her.

Her suggestion was that I did have the skills I needed, but that something was stopping me using them. Together we explored possible reasons, right back into my childhood. This helped me gain understanding of so much that had been unclear – my reactions, my assumptions, my thought patterns – myself. And the greater my understanding has become, the more I have been able to use it to challenge what comes instinctively to me, and to channel myself in the direction in which I want to move. It has been a voyage of self discovery in the process of which I have been amazed at the intimacy of God's love and care for me throughout the years. And I have found freedom. No longer am I hampered by the baggage I carried from my childhood years: the struggle to prove myself to God by being good, not making a fuss, being helpful and so on. His love is unconditional and unchanging. I know I am still in need, but my neediness is no longer a dark and damp abyss; there is something of the light and warmth of God's presence in it.

My story has not yet ended, and humanly speaking it does not look as though it will have a 'happy ever after' ending. But Jesus, who worked miracles while on earth, can still work them from his throne in heaven. He will perform his perfect sovereign will and bring glory to himself in the doing of it. 'And we know that in all things God works for the good of those who love him, who have been called according to his purpose' (Romans 8:28).

I still struggle at times with depression and loneliness – sometimes to the point when death seems a means of escape – but my times are in my loving Father's hands. I do not know the future regarding my marriage. My mother's increasing frailty makes me fearful, and the world appears increasingly godless and evil. At work I meet clients whose hopes have soured and whose dreams lie in shatters. Sometimes I feel overwhelmed by the pain of it all.

Hope for time and eternity
'Don't take your daughter home – she is not going to live.' Thankfully my parents ignored that advice. The heart problem that was evident when I was born has had corrective surgery on a number of occasions. Soon I will have further heart surgery, without which my quality of life would decrease quite markedly. I will commit myself into the skilled hands of an anaesthetist and a surgeon. I can do that with assurance, because I have already committed myself to the One who is able to do more than we ask or think, who will

keep me to all eternity, and who has promised never to leave me nor forsake me, and to guide me safely to my eternal home. In Isaiah 43:1 the Lord says: 'Fear not, for I have redeemed you, I have called you by name; you are mine.' And I believe him.

Just a few weeks after completing this chapter, Katie underwent major heart surgery from which she did not regain consciousness. She died six days later. For Katie, 'There will be no more death or mourning or crying or pain, for the old order of things has passed away' (Revelation 21:4).

12

JENNY AND ALASTAIR BROWN

God of grace and God of glory,
On thy people pour thy power;
Now fulfil thy Church's story;
Bring her bud to glorious flower.
Grant us wisdom, grant us courage,
For the facing of this hour.

This was our opening hymn at Glenmuick Church of Scotland, Ballater, on Sunday 24th January, 1988. During the singing the last line of that verse became a prayer as I felt increasingly unwell. A sore throat and cold earlier that month had left me sluggish, and now waves of dizziness swept over me. It was with great difficulty I remained standing. Struggling to concentrate during the prayer that followed, all I could do at its conclusion was utter a few words of apology before collapsing into my seat.

An hour later, although the pain in my shoulder and the tingling in my left hand remained, I was feeling a little better. I felt reassured too, having been examined by my family doctor. However, he thought it wise that I should be checked out, and shortly afterwards I was admitted to the Coronary Care Unit at Aberdeen Royal Infirmary.

Linked up to a monitor, feeling exhausted and a little apprehensive, was not the start to the second year of my ministry that I had imagined.

Later that afternoon Jenny, my wife, visited. She relayed messages from concerned members who had been present in church that morning, and brought the love of our boys, Andrew and Colin, who were no doubt wondering what was happening. Jenny's presence and her chat about the boys brought tears, and to lighten the moment she reminded me of my first and last experience of a hospital bed.

It was an oppressively hot and thundery evening in St Andrews when I visited Jenny as she was going into labour with Andrew. A fatal combination of heat, excitement, and another's pain left me weak at the knees, so much so that I was glad to accept a few minutes rest on the bed opposite Jenny! Tears and laughter, God-given emotions, are a potent mix, especially when life throws up the unexpected as that day certainly had. Jenny prayed, and not for the first time expressed what I felt but was unable to put into words. As she was leaving that night she quoted the words of Isaiah 40:31: 'Those who hope in the Lord will renew their strength. They will soar on wings like eagles; they will run and not grow weary, they will walk and not be faint.'

Thankfully the tests indicated no heart problems. Two days later, having recovered from thirteen minutes on the treadmill, I was discharged. The most likely cause of the problem was a virus, and the cure? – a couple of weeks' rest, then a return to work.

The problem persists
During the following weeks the anticipated recovery simply did not happen. The endless supply of energy I had always enjoyed, and now realised I had taken for granted, was severely rationed and, although most people did not realise it, I was exhausted to the point of collapse. On the Friday before Palm Sunday I finally admitted to myself that something was wrong that had to be investigated. We attended a school service during which a trophy was dedicated to the memory of Peter, a member of our Sunday School who had died tragically following a road accident the previous autumn. Afterwards in the home of Peter's parents, when I felt unwell a doctor present examined me but could find nothing wrong. Less than twenty four hours previously my own doctor had found nothing amiss when I became unwell while making a pastoral visit. I was again admitted to hospital for tests and observation.

The consultant diagnosed Post Viral Fatigue, and explained that it was also known as *Myalgic Encephalomyelitis*, ME for short. He explained the difficulty of treating the problem with conventional therapies as their success rate varied widely. Rest was the generally accepted regime, and he was rightly guarded when I asked how long I would be off work, although he suggested it would be several months at least. In fact, it was about two years before I was fit to return to full duties, and much was to happen in between. 'Grant us wisdom, grant us courage, for the facing of this hour.' With hindsight, it was indeed the ideal prayer for me.

Looking back

My early years growing up in Coatbridge were healthy and happy. I was an active and enthusiastic member of the Boys' Brigade. The teaching I received in the weekly Bible Class, and the attractive Christian example of the leaders, became the foundations from which my faith developed. Church, which once had been boring (not a word invented by today's teenagers!) was now interesting, and the Jesus of the gospels became real and alive with meaning. Our company was part of the local Free Church of Scotland, and the ministry of Rev Ken Cameron challenged me to accept new life in and through Jesus, and live his teaching.

I wanted to be a footballer on leaving school, but a distinct lack of skill put paid to that, and I trained instead as a draughtsman with an engineering company in Glasgow. And, when I completed my training in 1970, Jenny and I married. We shared a love of Christ. Her background was United Free Church and mine Free Church – we attended the Church of Scotland which was on our doorstep in Glenrothes. Eighteen months later the opportunity to live and work in Easter Ross presented itself, and the summer of 1972 was spent setting up home in Alness on the shores of the Cromarty Firth.

We settled quickly, and found ourselves very much at home in Rosskeen Church of Scotland. I soon became involved with the BB, and not long afterwards started teaching in Sunday School. Jenny had her hands full too, what with her church activities and the arrival of Andrew's baby brother, Colin. Later I became an elder in that church around which our lives revolved. We felt God's hand had brought us north, and only his will would move us away. But deep down we 'knew' we would never move on ... or so we thought.

In the spring of 1977 we had planned a holiday week in London. A few days before we were due to leave I had a phone call from an ex-colleague wanting to know if I would be interested in a job in Aberdeen. The company was London based and I agreed to go for an interview while on holiday, but with little expectation. A letter offering me the job awaited our return. We prayed over this and were still unsure when, a few days later, I had to attend a residential computer course. Each night we discussed the matter on the phone. God ruled, and overruled, and a few months later we moved to Kintore, twelve miles from Aberdeen where I started work.

Here I am. Send me.

Two and a half years later we attended an evening service during which divinity students spoke of their calls to the ministry. I had been wondering if I should consider specifically Christian work. The service ended and, although I found the talks interesting, I felt no compelling call. In the moments of quiet after the service the organist played a hymn much beloved of generations of Boys' Brigade members, 'Will your anchor hold in the storms of life?' At that point I knew deep inside myself that God was calling me to Christian service, perhaps to the ministry. Within a few months, at the age of thirty, I was studying for a Bachelor of Divinity Degree at Aberdeen University. Some people may have thought that I overreacted to a few notes of a hymn tune, but I had the sure conviction that God spoke to me.

In September 1986 I was ordained at Ballater and settled quickly into the routine of ministry. The church members were supportive. And the thriving Sunday School, with its dedicated leadership, was supplemented by a youth group led by Jenny. We all made new friends and began to settle in the community. It was a major move for Andrew and Colin with a mid-term change of school and the leaving of friends they had known for almost as long as they could remember. We started doing a little hill walking and I played football for the local team during the summer. A family boating holiday on the Norfolk Broads was the highlight of the year. With 1987 coming to a close, I was thankful for the past and enthusiastic about the future; with plans for both the family and the church – plans that the events of 24th January were to scupper as ME took over, and dominated our lives.

The diagnosis of ME meant very little in terms of understanding the illness. But, in terms of what I could do, it controlled my life completely. I had always been relatively fit, and this I put down to my daily swim. Now, having been bed-bound for several weeks, the short distance to the toilet was as far as I could manage. Mentally and physically exhausted, my system shut down, and what happened during those weeks is a blur. As I emerged slowly from this hibernation the reality of what was happening to me began to sink in. Growing in understanding, I discovered more about ME when the BBC programme *Horizon* featured it and told the story of some sufferers. Michael Mayne, the Dean of Westminster, had ME and in time made a good recovery. Others were still ill years later and showed little sign of progress. Optimistic as ever, I believed that I would soon get better and return to my duties.

After all, God had called me into the ministry, surely it was his intention that I should minister.

Summer and autumn came and went and, as 1989 began, I felt that my health would surely improve. By the end of March I saw the first positive sign of this when I walked about five hundred yards one Friday afternoon. I was delighted, but came down to earth quickly the next day when, totally exhausted, I was confined to bed. For a short time I had glimpsed what could be, and tears of frustration followed. The words of Isaiah, which had been for so long a comfort, now hung over me, and inward cries of 'have I not waited long enough for my strength to be renewed?' found that the answer was NO.

My first sermon in Glenmuick had been based on Psalm 46:10: 'Be still, and know that I am God.' Being confined within four walls gave me plenty of time to be still and to find and know what God was doing in and through my experience. I had read or heard somewhere the phrase 'spiritual sunbathing', and that was what I attempted to do. My efforts to 'get up and go' had failed; my strength had let me down and I now rested in God's strength. A verse from the Bible, a line from a Christian song, these were my meditations. Spiritual rest suggests inactivity, but for me it was a time when God actively enabled me to accept what was happening, and to find strength for what lay ahead. I had preached on the subject to others, now I was preaching to myself. As the prophet Isaiah says: 'In quietness and in trust is your strength' (Isaiah 30:15).

Those who experience long term illness can become obsessed with their problems. And I was no different. A simple enquiry about how I was doing might receive a detailed breakdown of hours slept, time sitting observing, yards walked. I think I could, and often did, risk being boring, as each twinge and feeling became the subject of in-depth analysis. Everything revolved around me and I was unaware of the strain that Jenny was beginning to feel; left, as she was, running our home, coping with church matters, and working part time as a nurse.

Together in trouble

By the middle of July Jenny was attending the doctor. Breathlessness, discomfort when both sitting up and lying down, and mild chest pains caused concern. A hospital appointment was arranged and I insisted on driving her to Aberdeen. We set off. Having covered two of the forty two miles of the journey I had to stop the car, exhausted. When I was safely in bed Jenny left for the city with a friend, and on her return she too was confined to bed.

Occasionally someone called at the manse whom we had not seen for a number of years. That Sunday three visitors arrived at the door, and in each case eighteen years had passed since our last meeting. We were both in bed when a lunch time caller rang the bell. Jenny got up and answered the door. I could hear in the distance my aunt's voice. Some time after I heard the door closing I got up to see why Jenny had not come back to bed, only to discover her lying at the top of the stairs. Our doctor was called, and before long Jenny was on her way back to Aberdeen, this time by ambulance, suffering from what turned out to be a virus of some sort. Later that evening, as darkness fell, I answered a knock at the door to find a stranger standing there ... or so I thought. Eighteen years previously he had been a few pounds lighter and clean shaven, though now he sported a full beard, yet the voice, when he spoke, was instantly recognisable. It was Ken Cameron, my boyhood minister. Being in the area to visit a Free Church camp he had decided to call, quite unaware of the happenings of the day. His was a welcome visit indeed.

A few minutes later Mary, one of the girls from Ken's Coatbridge youth fellowship, now a leader at the camp he was visiting, joined us. Jenny has often since made a joke of it. She was in hospital just a few hours and there I was entertaining a girl I had known many years before! Not for the first time my mother-in-law arrived to take charge of home and family. A week later Jenny was home.

My recovery did take place, although it was slow in happening. After what had seemed forever, I returned to full time ministry in March 1990. But a year later, just as I thought the worst was over, I took a cold, then shingles which left me drained. Resting over the summer failed to restore my health and, with no sign of recovery being forthcoming, I resigned from my ministry at Glenmuick. The congregation allowed us to remain in the manse over the winter and we prayed about our future accommodation.

On the move

Through a chance meeting with a member of another church, who just then heard about our situation, God answered our prayers in a remarkable way. The phone call that followed led to an invitation to view a large house which, if we wanted it, was ours to rent. My brother, a painter and decorator, prepared the house for us and, in March 1992, we moved into the presbytery house attached to Ballater's Roman Catholic Church, previously occupied by the parish priest. Coming from the West of Scotland, our move surprised some of those from the same background, but we were delighted and felt God showed humour as well as kindness in his provision for our needs.

We stayed there for sixteen months until a new priest arrived. Six months in a friend's house followed then we moved back to Kintore. Life had turned full circle, but at last we were settled. In all we had lived in seven houses in eight years, and packing and unpacking had become a family pastime. Every box had a number and this information was stored on computer. But what box contained the computer? In answer to our earnest prayers we found ourselves settled once again.

Since returning to Kintore I have shown a little improvement. Over the years I have discovered what I can and cannot do, and how to manage the energy I have. An analogy would be a bank account in which sleep and rest keeps me in credit. If I attempt too much I spend more than I have, and the penalty for being on the debit side is days in bed spent slowly building up an energy balance.

I have been asked by friends if I would return to the ministry should my health improve. My usual response is to wonder if anyone would have me with a track record like mine. A perceptive friend might say, and perhaps rightly so, that I have failed to answer the question. Perhaps it is that I don't really want to think about it, for I treasured my time as minister of Glenmuick, and it was a joy to serve the Lord in that capacity and a sad day when I had to resign.

What I have written no more than covers the bare facts of how an illness upset one family's plans. ME has meant major changes in our lives, with Jenny working full-time and my role that of houseperson. Someone, knowing that the title did not appeal to me at all, suggested that I call myself a domestic engineer. But, throughout all the changes, the love of God has carried us through, and many people have been used in a ministry of encouragement.

I am his, and he is mine
In my daily Bible reading notes a year or so ago, I read the words: 'All wind blows us towards God's goal'. Life has thrown much in our direction that we would have chosen to avoid. But, like Paul, who prayed three times that his thorn in the flesh be removed, we have found God's answer is that his grace is sufficient for all our needs (2 Corinthians 12:7ff.). Michael Mayne, Dean of Westminster, wrote: 'Jesus did not offer people perfect health and a painless death. Human minds are fragile and vulnerable. What he offers is eternal life: a new relationship with God of such a quality that nothing that may happen to us can destroy it. And it is that kind of confidence and trust in God, come what may, which is the true healing of the human spirit.'

The title of his book is *A Year Lost and Found*, and that sums up much of what I feel about my experience of ME. I have found a strength I preached about. I have experienced the peace that I preached. And I have enjoyed the presence of

189

the Lord that I so often commended to my people, and found it to a depth that I had not understood before. In that sense the years of ME have been growing years, with roots growing ever deeper into the experience of God's eternal love and of the human love of my darling wife, both in sickness and in health.

Some time ago I was given a card on which was a morning prayer. It sits beside our bed still, encouraging me with its words: 'Lord, help me to remember that nothing is going to happen to me today that you and I together can't handle.'

Irene Howat lives in Argyllshire where her husband Angus is a minister of the Free Church of Scotland. Among many other activities Irene edits the denomination's monthly children's magazine, *The Instructor*.

For many years Irene has had to live with permanent pain, and she describes what this has meant to herself and her family in her book, *Pain My Companion*. In addition Irene has written *When the Thornbush Blooms,* designed to help people facing difficult situations. Irene also edited *Light in the Middle of the Tunnel*, a collection of testimonies of personal suffering, all of whom discovered that God brought his grace into their lives. These titles are published by Christian Focus.